WHAT OTHE
ABOUT

M000033716

"I'm so proud of Drew and his willingness to share difficult experiences in an authentic and helpful way. This book is an important reminder that each of us has a mission in life and we can fulfill it as long as we turn to the right source, get up when we fall down, and keep moving forward in faith."

—*Jane Clayson Johnson*, journalist and best-selling author, *Silent Souls Weeping*

"As a therapist, I've seen firsthand how mental illness, discouragement, and other challenges are misunderstood and stigmatized in Latter-day Saint culture. Drew's story, written with vulnerability and honesty, gives readers permission to discover and fully live their own missions—regardless of the personal battles they face. To anyone who is looking for understanding, hope, and healing, I highly recommend Drew's book, *The Meaning of Your Mission.*"

—*Julie de Azevedo Hanks*, PhD, LCSW, therapist, author, owner of Wasatch Family Therapy, assistant professor of social work at Utah Valley University

"Drew's honesty and openness will bless many young adults whose full-time missions may have been altered by world conditions or personal circumstances. In addition, Drew's experience is an encouragement to discover that a full-time mission is only a small subset of a life's mission for each individual, which is ongoing and unique, and from which one will never be released."

—*John Bytheway,* author

"The author poses the question, 'Why not memorize the First Vision by singing it?' Drew Young asks the reader to find his or her own voice as he tells the parable of his song of discovery. Through his personal reflection with cultural conflict and awareness of his internal struggle surrounding a mission call, he claims his own path of reconciliation to *believe Christ*. He recounts a journey beyond the expected mission experience, transitioning from anxiety and despair to acceptance and fulfillment. With integrity, he grows with experience, singing his journey to the music of his own creation. I invite you to listen."

—*Richard C. Ferre,* MD, leading psychiatrist, Family Services Missionary Clinic, The Church of Jesus Christ of Latter-Day Saints

"Finally, someone who isn't afraid to be real and raw about the not-so-pretty and complex aspects of our life's mission. We strive to be the person we believe we are supposed to be, but it can be discouraging and isolating when we fall short. Being in a culture that values image and perfection, it can be difficult to handle the reality of how messy and imperfect our lives truly are. Often times because of the judgment of others or the harsh judgment we have toward ourselves, we don't see our intrinsic value. Drew's book helps validate that experience and draw up purpose and direction out of any situation, especially when it isn't deemed the 'perfect ideal' experience. He shows that mental illness, trials, confusion, and conflict can be a jumping off point for connection and a more fulfilling life. If you have ever felt alone or like you aren't enough, give this a read."

—*Monica Moore Smith,* film actress, content creator, and writer

"*The Meaning of Your Mission* is such an important topic. God's plan of happiness is personal for each of His children, so it is heartbreaking when we compare our plan with someone else's. Thank you, Drew, for sharing such an authentic look into the wrestle and process of finding your way when the way looks different than planned."

—*Ganel-Lyn Condie,* speaker and best-selling author

"Drew's book reiterates the truth that the Savior has already taken care of it. Stop worrying so much about being perfect. Jesus bought us with His blood. To think we are anything less than that is to undervalue the sacrifice of our Lord on our behalf."

—*Paul Cardall,* Gospel Music Association's Dove Award-winning recording artist

"In *The Meaning of Your Mission,* Drew Young has written a valuable book to help lessen stigma associated with anxiety, depression, and having your mission cut shorter than anticipated. He helps people understand needed perspectives that help—and hurt—the wonderful missionaries who experience this challenge. This book has so much to learn, but in particular I felt drawn in by Drew's transparent rawness with his experience, and benefitted by the principles he shares to help us understand and know how to help someone dealing with similar experiences."

—*Anthony Sweat,* associate professor, Brigham Young University, Department of Church History and Doctrine

"I came home early from my mission about five years ago on an honorable release, but I struggled with so much anxiety about my decision to come home. I wish I'd had this book at the time. Drew speaks about how Heavenly Father still loves us immensely for the sacrifices we make, no matter what they are. I am so glad that this issue is finally being spoken about and addressed for today's missionaries!"

—*Jane Williamson*, Latter-day Saint Instagram influencer, @janeinsane

"One challenge faced by many in our community is the difficulty of returning early from missionary service, either personally or helping a loved one who has. This book provides increased understanding and personal perspective on this challenging issue and provides important insights to consider."

—*John Hilton III*, associate professor, BYU Religious Education

"At first, I was skeptical of this book's ability to provide deep, meaningful advice and experiences for early returned missionaries. However, Drew shares his raw emotions and stories about this 'hush-hush' topic in a way that embraces all who read it as well as empowers those who have lived it. As a big advocate of sisters serving missions, I especially loved the chapter where Drew directly addresses the young adult women of the Church and discusses the differences between the doctrinal and cultural expectations that often plague our faith. I highly recommend this to ALL members. If you're thinking about serving, *The Meaning of Your Mission* will give you direction and help you discover your purpose before you step foot into the field. And if you're just living your life's mission, Drew's book will help you in your own walk with Christ, along with helping you understand and feel compassion for members who are often struggling in silence."

—*Jesse Espinosa*, Latter-day Saint YouTube influencer, @SundayJess

"After teaching the author in my college course, I hired him to work with me. I was impressed with his determination, ability, and genuine interest in other people. It was not until many months later that I learned of his struggles. What makes *The Meaning of Your Mission* different is that it is more than just his story. It provides a guiding light for others who struggle and seek solace in life. It is not just a road map to be followed but also provides hope for others to find their personal way to happiness. This story is real, and for those who have feelings of inadequacy, it offers insight into the beauty of finding our path even if it is sometimes filled with feelings that don't have to defeat us. What I loved was the way he showed that with all the issues he faced, he kept moving and found the way that was right for him. This message can be read and assimilated into the lives of those who ponder his thoughts and use them to develop their own ideas of a future. He gives hope that struggles are places to start the process, not definitions of the person. I firmly believe that his experience was a vital outcome of his missionary service."

—*Kerry Hammock*, director, University Advisement
Center, Brigham Young University

"I am so grateful that Drew was willing to share such personal and painful experiences in *The Meaning of Your Mission*. I know that this book will be a huge blessing to other young people who may not be able to serve a mission in the way they anticipated, as well as their parents, leaders, and anyone who may be struggling with feelings of perfectionism or self-doubt."

—*Vanessa Quigley*, cofounder, Chatbooks

"In *The Meaning of Your Mission*, Drew lays out with striking vulnerability his coming-of-age story. If you are a member of The Church of Jesus Christ of Latter-day Saints and you (or someone you know) struggles with discouragement or mental illness, Drew's heartfelt memoir will provide both comfort and encouragement."

—*Whitney Johnson,* award-winning author, world-class
keynote speaker, frequent lecturer for Harvard
Business School's Executive Education, and
an executive coach and advisor to CEOs

"In these distracting and contentious times, we are often bombarded with disparate messages about who we are and what the meaning of our lives should be. This heartfelt, poignant, and insightful book points the reader to a deeper and more meaningful life. As someone who struggled with intense feelings of depression after my mission, I wish I had been able to read this book then. As it is, I am profoundly grateful for those who will now benefit from Young's inspired research and writing."

—*Seth Adam Smith*, author and mental health and suicide prevention advocate

the
MEANING
of YOUR
MISSION

the MEANING *of* YOUR MISSION

LESSONS & PRINCIPLES
TO KNOW YOU ARE ENOUGH

DREW YOUNG

CFI
AN IMPRINT OF CEDAR FORT, INC.
SPRINGVILLE, UTAH

ISBN 13: 978-1-4621-3806-7

Published by CFI, an imprint of Cedar Fort, Inc.
2373 W. 700 S., Springville, UT 84663
Distributed by Cedar Fort, Inc., www.cedarfort.com

LIBRARY OF CONGRESS CONTROL NUMBER: 2020938116

Cover design by Shawnda T. Craig
Cover design © 2020 Cedar Fort, Inc.

Printed in the United States of America

10 9 8 7 6 5 4 3 2 1

Printed on acid-free paper

DEDICATION

To my dear friends who feel like they aren't loved, don't measure up, or can never be good enough—this is for you.

CONTENTS

Contents

FOREWORD

In 1987, Emily Perl Kingsley wrote the now famous poem "Holland."[1]

It describes the experience of having everyone planning a trip to Italy. Everyone you know loves Italy. They plan, prepare, and go. You also cannot wait to go to Italy. You pack your bags and get on the plane. As you land, you get the announcement, "Welcome to Holland!"

"Holland!" you exclaim. "But I bought a ticket to Italy! I packed for Italy. Everyone I know has gone to Italy."

But Kingsley goes on to write how you planned for one but got another. You have to buy new guidebooks. You must meet new and different people. You expected one thing and you got something different. You expected Italy but in Holland you must stay.

You meet new friends and learn to love Holland. Holland has windmills and tulips. It even has Rembrandts. Everyone you know is bragging about Italy, and it hurts to hear about it. "I planned on going to Italy," you say. But you learn to love Holland.

The poem reminds us that we often expect and plan for one thing, and often we receive something special, beautiful, but very different.

You may have had a similar experience with your mission. Perhaps you envisioned serving for two years or eighteen months on a mission in an exotic locale, speaking a new language with fluency. Maybe it seemed that everyone you know was doing exactly that, and you were excited to join in. But then your life took an unexpected turn. Illness, difficulty, a pandemic, a family situation, or another circumstance completely altered your path. You wanted to go to Italy, but found out the Lord was sending you to Holland instead.

And as Kingsley wisely wrote, "The important thing is that they haven't taken you to a horrible, disgusting, and filthy place . . . it is just a different place."

You may feel that you've had your world turned upside down. You may wonder if you were supposed to go on a mission in the first place. You may second-guess your ability to receive personal revelation. Slow down and take a deep breath. We have Heavenly Parents and a Savior who know everything. They knew what would happen long before you did. They know how this all ends up playing out.

As you let go of your expectations and allow the Lord to guide you, your new path will become more and more beautiful to you. Elder Jeffrey Holland taught,

> Every experience can become a redemptive experience if we remain bonded to our Father in Heaven through it. These difficult lessons teach us that man's extremity is God's opportunity, and if we will be humble and faithful, if we will be believing and not curse God for our problems, He can turn the unfair and inhumane and debilitating prisons of our lives into temples—or at least into circumstance that can bring comfort and revelation, divine companionship and peace.[1]

Trust in heaven means we must also trust in heaven's timing. You are on the right track. If you keep moving forward, asking for guidance, and keep working toward good things, you'll end up exactly where you are supposed to end up.

In this book, Drew Young relates his personal story of his mission being different than he had planned and prepared for. He reminds us that a loving Father in Heaven knows his children perfectly and only gives good gifts. Luke teaches,

> For every one that asketh receiveth; and he that seeketh findeth; and to him that knocketh, it shall be opened. If a son shall ask bread of any of you that is a father, will he give him a stone, or if he ask a fish, will he for a fish give him a serpent? Or if he ask an egg will he offer him a scorpion? (Luke 11:10)

The Lord gives his children good gifts. If we ask, we will find them! If we ask for nourishment (bread), He will give us fish or something more than we ask. He won't give us something dangerous (scorpion) or garbage (a rock). We may expect to serve in one place and serve another. We may expect to serve a certain length of time, but the Lord may have something in mind. It is important to remember that Heavenly Father gives only good gifts.

The Lord sends us where we need to serve, when we need to serve, and for the time we need to serve. We may expect Italy, and we may receive Holland, but as Young in this book reminds us, "Your mission awaits."

Drew Young has written an important, helpful book for every future or current missionary. More books like this need to be written. Drew reminds us of important truths and writes with honesty and vigor. I am grateful that he has written this book, and I see it as part of his mission.

—Dr. Henry "Hank" Smith
April 2020

NOTES

1. "Welcome to Holland"; see en.wikipedia.org/wiki/Welcome_to_Holland. Accessed June 15, 2020.
2. "Lessons from Liberty Jail," CES fireside, Brigham Young University, Sept. 7, 2008.

INTRODUCTION

Dear Elder Young,

You are hereby called to serve as a missionary for The Church of Jesus Christ of Latter-day Saints. You are assigned to labor in the Baltic Mission. In addition to your calling to serve, you will be assigned to labor in the Estonia mission region.

Those words popped off the page at me like they were bolded, italicized, and underlined. *Estonia!* I thought. *Where is that?* For those who had to draw the world map in middle school, Estonia might've been easy to spot, but I had completely forgotten. My mother literally fell to the ground in absolute shock of where the Lord would be sending her youngest child for two years—or so she thought. My head soon found its way onto her shoulders where the excitement, nervousness, and humble gratitude of what had just taken place softly turned into tears that coursed down my cheeks.

I always knew the Lord had a specific plan for me. Just three weeks prior to receiving that call to serve, I was told by the missionary department that I would need to wait six months before I could be recommended for missionary service. I had just returned home from work to see my mom sitting outside on the porch. This was unusual, because she only sat on that specific spot if, (A), I had done something wrong, covered it up secretly, and then she found out about it, or (B), she had something urgent to tell me. This instance proved to be a "B" moment. I asked her what was wrong, and she responded that she had just gotten off the phone with someone at the missionary department. Upon viewing my missionary application, they had discovered some medical red flags that I had disclosed. She then said, "Drew, they told me that you will have to wait six months before you can resubmit your application. They want to make sure your medical problems are taken care of and you can function as a missionary."

The word *devastated* didn't even come close to what I was feeling.

There I was, desiring to serve the Lord in the best way I knew how. This feeling of a lack of control was crippling. Putting my future in the hands of someone I trusted, yet knowing I would be responsible for following them, was difficult. This lack of control would become detrimental to my conversion and progress over the next two years as I would quickly discover that there are certain things in life that we *can't* control. That was hard for me to accept since I was one to take the initiative, obey, and strive to serve to the best of my ability.

I believe there are heavenly attributes that must be developed if we wish to become like our Heavenly Parents.

As those words came out of my mother's mouth, I realized something. You can bear testimony and post on social media that you have faith in the Lord and in His timing, but until that faith is tested, it's only words. If you have a gun, faith makes up the barrel, gunpowder, bullet, and person holding it (all essential). But what use is that gun unless you have a finger to pull the trigger? Action is that finger. Action is what will bring the gun to its full use and potential.

We can have our scriptures. We can have our missionary plaque. We can even have a temple recommend, but until we *act*, those are only objects. Faith leads to action. Action leads to conversion.

I hiked up the stairs, entered my room, slammed the door shut, and threw my keys on the ground. What came to my mind next was the story of President Hugh B. Brown, formerly a member of the Quorum of the Twelve Apostles and a counselor in the First Presidency. Upon enlisting in the Canadian Army, he worked hard and received high ranks and admiration from his superiors. He was in line to receive a promotion, but it was denied him because he was a Latter-day Saint. After hearing this news, President Brown relates his own experience:

> I got on the train and started back . . . with a broken heart, with bitterness in my soul. . . . When I got to my tent, . . . I threw my cap on the cot. I clenched my fists, and I shook them at heaven. I said, "How could you do this to me, God? I have done everything I could do to measure up. There is nothing that I could have done—that I should have done—that I haven't done. How could you do this to me?" I was as bitter as gall.

And then I heard a voice, and I recognized the tone of this voice. It was my own voice, and the voice said, "I am the gardener here. I know what I want you to do." The bitterness went out of my soul, and I fell on my knees by the cot to ask forgiveness for my ungratefulness. . . .

And now, almost 50 years later, I look up to [God] and say, "Thank you, Mr. Gardener, for cutting me down, for loving me enough to hurt me."[1]

Though my situation didn't happen fifty years ago, the meaning of his words carries the same importance to me. My words are President Brown's. Humbly and sincerely declaring, "Thy will be done," and then following the Savior with sincerity, will bring more peace to the human soul than anything this world can offer. Though the Lord may chasten us, He does so because He has much greater blessings prepared for us if we humbly and faithfully wait upon Him. (See Mosiah 23:21–22.)

I took that experience in my room and carried it with me to college a couple of weeks later. I trusted in God that He would provide what I could not understand. During the first week of school, I walked out of my apartment for my nine o'clock class. As I closed the door, I felt my phone vibrate. I looked down to discover a text from my bishop back home. It read, "Drew, your mission call has been assigned. You should receive it this week."

What? I thought. *How could this be possible?* Just two weeks before, I felt dejected and believed I would be required to wait six months before submitting mission papers again. Nevertheless, I believe God heard my humble call of "Thy will be done" and deemed it appropriate to offer me the opportunity to serve him earlier than expected.

That phrase, "Thy will be done," would come to mean more to me than any other four words in the English language. Over the next two years, I would battle acute anxiety and depression. I would struggle through panic attacks, thoughts of suicide, countless doctor appointments, and nights filled with prayer offered through teary eyes, muffled speech, and a broken heart. I would come to understand why it is never wise to make preconceived judgments and that we never know the whole story behind why someone acts the way they do. I learned that it's not up to us to be the final judge. It's up to us to love and be compassionate and kind.

This is my personal account of how the Savior can convert anyone, anytime, and anywhere if they offer their hearts to Him. I am an early returned missionary, and I couldn't be more thankful to the Lord for blessing me with my health *opportunities*, because in His own words, "This will I do that ye may stand as witnesses for me hereafter, and that ye may know of a surety that I, the Lord God, do visit my people in their afflictions" (Mosiah 24:14).

Though this book comes from my perspective as an early returned missionary and will include several stories pertaining to my own missionary experiences, the application is universal. The lessons, stories, and principles taught within the following pages are for everyone as they seek to understand what their mission is, both in life and within the Church. For young adults, converts, nonmembers, those plagued by mental or emotional illness, those whose minds are clouded by despair and discouragement, those struggling with their faith or with keeping the commandments, those who find the Latter-day Saint culture difficult to understand and live, and especially those who may feel that no matter how hard they try, they're just not good enough—may you feel the peace and assurance that comes from knowing that the Lord has much in store for you. You are loved. You are needed. Your mission awaits you.

NOTE

1. Hugh B. Brown, "The Currant Bush," *Liahona*, Mar. 2002, 22, 24; *New Era*, Jan. 1973, 14, 15. As cited in "As Many as I love, I rebuke and Chasten," D. Todd Christofferson, *Ensign*, May 2011.

CHAPTER 1

THE WHAT AND WHY OF MISSIONARY SERVICE

THE WHAT OF MISSIONARY SERVICE

President Dallin H. Oaks said, "What we call '. . . missionary work' is not a program, but an attitude of love and outreach to those around us."[1]

In The Church of Jesus Christ of Latter-day Saints, there is such an emphasis on the term *missionary work* that people forget *what* missionary work is. As President Oaks said, it isn't a program, and it isn't a checklist item. It is love. It is hope. It is faith. It is, as Alma tells us, being willing to mourn with those who mourn and to comfort those who stand in need of comfort (Mosiah 18:9). One word in that passage is more important than all the rest: *willing.* The Lord doesn't command us to do something with no help provided, no hope promised, and no blessings offered if we fall short. He rewards those who are willing to serve, regardless of the length or perceived impact that service has. People describe their life as a mission. If that is the case, are the only ones who succeed the ones who live the longest or garner the most social media acclaim? Of course not. What we do with the time and opportunities given to us is what matters.

A BRIEF SHOUT-OUT TO MY EARLY RETURNED MISSIONARY FRIENDS

Alma 40:8 states, "All is as one day with God, and time is only measured unto man." Yes, a Latter-day Saint mission is "typically" twenty-four or eighteen months, but those who *cannot* serve that allotted length of time need not grow weary, for they are laying the foundation of a great work.

What is that work? It's their salvation, their future, their hopes and dreams, and a lifetime of service, however long that lifetime may be.

Elder Dieter F. Uchtdorf encouraged those going through this situation when he said,

> Many of our missionaries have prepared themselves from childhood on to serve a mission. They decided on their own free will that they wanted to go. And then they accepted the call from the Prophet of God to serve as a disciple of Jesus Christ, as a representative of the Savior, wherever the Lord would assign them for however long.
>
> There have been other times in history when missionaries have had unexpected releases—due to health concerns, accidents, war, or other circumstances. The key points are the decision to go and the decision to accept.
>
> Everything that happens after that is often influenced by circumstances not within the decision of the missionary. You prepared, you accepted the call, and you gave your best. That is what counts. That is what makes all the difference. That is what makes a missionary.[2]

Have you ever felt discouraged because even though you were trying your very best to do the right thing, someone else was getting noticed, or you weren't feeling like the good you were doing really made a difference?

I'm here to tell you that it doesn't matter who *sees* your service or the good you do. What matters is that you serve and *do good*.

When I returned home after sixty-three days of service, I was fatigued, ill, and discouraged. I didn't have anyone to turn to, and I didn't know what to do next with my life. Was I successful? Did I fail the Lord and my family? This question brought me to a mental and emotional collapse. Because of this experience, I sought professional help. I met two men I perceive as angels. They changed my perspective on missionary work and service in general. They ultimately shaped my full mental and emotional recovery. One of those men, whom I will call Jake, was my counselor. Jake was blessed through various callings in the Church to stay close to the Lord. Through his professional duties, he had the opportunity to take care of people like me who were struggling.

A few weeks into my visits with him, I couldn't get past the belief that I had let everyone down by returning early from my mission.

"This wasn't part of *my* plan," I exclaimed with tears in my eyes. "I failed. I feel terrible."

Jake responded calmly, "Drew, let's open the scriptures. Have you heard of Oliver Granger?"

I shook my head. I had never heard of Oliver Granger, though I would quickly learn why the Lord decided to include him in the scriptures. It is, in part, because of Oliver Granger that I made it to where I am today. He helped me understand how the Lord defines "success."

Oliver wasn't well known among the Saints. He never saw many "numbers" and didn't accumulate any public acclaim during his earthly life or in his service to others. Yet, the Lord held him, and continues to hold him, in high esteem.

"I remember my servant Oliver Granger; behold, verily I say unto him that his name shall be had in sacred remembrance from generation to generation, forever and ever, saith the Lord" (D&C 117:12).

President Boyd K. Packer described Oliver Granger's standing in the Church when he explained,

> Oliver Granger was a very ordinary man. He was mostly blind having "lost his sight by cold and exposure" (*History of the Church*, 4:408). The First Presidency described him as "a man of the most strict integrity and moral virtue; and in fine, to be a man of God" (*History of the Church*, 3:350).
>
> When the Saints were driven from Kirtland, Ohio, in a scene that would be repeated in Independence, Far West, and in Nauvoo, Oliver was left behind to sell their properties for what little he could. There was not much chance that he could succeed. And, really, he did not succeed!
>
> But the Lord said, "Let him contend earnestly for the redemption of the First Presidency of my Church, saith the Lord; and when he falls he shall rise again, for his sacrifice shall be more sacred unto me than his increase, saith the Lord" (D&C 117:13).[3]

"For his *sacrifice* shall be more sacred unto me than his increase, saith the Lord" (emphasis added, D&C 117:13).

With those words, the Lord teaches a lesson to all who have "tried but fallen short" or have felt discouraged in their service to others.

First, it's not a matter of *if* we will fall but *when*, and when we fall, we will rise again.

Second, our sacrifice matters more to Him than the results (increase) we achieve.

We are promised that our joy will be great if we bring just one soul unto God. That one soul is our own (D&C 18:15).

So, take heart and be grateful. The Lord told Oliver Granger he was enough. He can tell you that too.

What does a mission *really* mean? What does service *really* mean? It means being willing to love. It means being willing to have faith and hope. It means that you trust in the Lord enough to say, "I may not have given you a lot of results, but I did give you a lot of heart. In fact, I gave you all my heart."

And with arms outstretched, a heart full of love, and the utmost gratitude for your service, He stands before you proclaiming, "Well done, good and faithful servant; thou hast been faithful over a few things, I will make thee ruler over many things: enter thou into the joy of thy lord" (Matthew 25:23).

THE WHY OF MISSIONARY SERVICE

Having been reminded that missionary service, or service of any kind, is simply an attitude of love and fellowship, the question remains, why serve a mission? Or, more specifically, why serve at all?

In the story of the good Samaritan, a Jewish man was traveling the road from Jerusalem to Jericho by himself. As he was traveling, a group of thieves came out of their hiding places and beat him, stole his clothes, took his money, and left him for dead. People passed by him as he lay on the ground in a state of unconsciousness. One man, a priest, looked down from his horse as he rode by but didn't stop. The second one, a Levite, dropped a few coins by the motionless body and moved on. Last, a Samaritan came by with his donkey. He looked upon the man with empathy and love. He poured oil into his wounds, wiped blood from his forehead, and gave him something to drink. He then dropped his own supplies on the side of the road, put the man on his donkey, and walked to the nearest village where he paid an innkeeper to take care of him until he was healed.

What's the moral of this story? Two things. First, it's important to mention that both the priest and the Levite were highly respected religious leaders. They were considered by the people to be close to God and able to hear and proclaim His word. They were powerful and influential. Yet, even with all the acclaim they had and the following they enjoyed, when it came time to live their faith and serve someone in need, they turned away. It seems that without an audience to impress, they thought it wasn't worth it.

On the other hand, the Samaritan that aided the man had no expectation to do so. Jewish people and Samaritan's didn't correspond or get along during that time, but that didn't matter. This was a man who lived what he believed and cared more about helping someone than being noticed for it.

Ironic, isn't it, that two thousand years later, the man who didn't serve to impress an audience is the one who is noticed and most esteemed?

President Thomas S. Monson taught,

> Each of us, in the journey through mortality, will travel his own Jericho Road. What will be your experience? What will be mine? Will I fail to notice him who has fallen among thieves and requires my help? Will you?
>
> Will I be one who sees the injured and hears his plea, yet crosses to the other side? Will you?
>
> Or will I be one who sees, who hears, who pauses, and who helps? Will you?
>
> Jesus provided our watchword, "Go, and do thou likewise." When we obey that declaration, there opens to our eternal view a vista of joy seldom equaled and never surpassed.[4]

Why do we serve? Because through it we experience "joy seldom equaled, and never surpassed."

Now, I have never met returned missionaries who said that their missions were easy, and many missionaries understand the *how* of a mission. They understand how to apply for a mission, they understand how to pack for a mission, and most of the time, they understand how to serve a mission. Many missionaries, however, never internalize that the *why* of a mission goes far beyond learning how to work, speaking a foreign language, or reading more scriptures.

Elder Uchtdorf explained, "While understanding the 'what' and 'how' of the gospel is necessary, the eternal fire and majesty of the gospel springs from the 'why.'"[5]

I love the imagery represented by a fire. Fire provides warmth and protection from the cold and dangers of life. Upon touching its crackling flame, we immediately jump, and adrenaline starts flowing through our bodies. Introduced to other substances, it spreads quickly. That is the same with the gospel, or, more specifically, with a mission. Its purpose is to provide all with a knowledge of Jesus Christ, missionaries and investigators alike. It gives an opportunity to feel of His warmth and protection. It ignites a feeling of awe and produces within us the adrenaline to be better. When shared, it can spread rapidly.

Yes, understanding "how" to serve and "what" serving means is important, but when we internalize the "why" of serving the Master, our lives take on an entirely new sense of meaning and wonder.

Elder Uchtdorf also stated, "The what and how . . . mark the way and keep us on the right path. The why . . . sanctifies our actions, transforming the mundane into the majestic. It magnifies our small acts of obedience into holy acts of consecration."[6]

We serve because we love God! We are grateful to Him for all He has given us. My dad is my exemplar when it comes to understanding the purpose of service in the gospel. He grew up in Brigham City, Utah, with two loving, hard-working parents. His mother spent most of her days on her feet as a waitress, and his father served in World War II and as a principal of a high school. There was no backtalk in his home. The chores were to be done before play, and no dishes were to be left in the sink after dinner. Every summer, my grandparents would send my dad to a ranch somewhere in Northern Utah to herd sheep, move sprinkler pipe, and irrigate. Why? Because his mother discerned that his friends were not engaged in activities that would benefit him, and she couldn't have been more correct. Some four decades later, most of those friends had committed suicide, overdosed on drugs, or died from alcohol abuse.

Listen to your mothers!

Those summer months, though hot, dirty, and laborious, molded my dad into an industrious, conscientious, and careful young man.

Because my dad's father smoked, drank, and didn't attend church very often, his mother set the example in the family for why living the gospel was important and why serving others was noble.

After graduating high school, my dad attended one year at Utah State University and then submitted his mission papers. He recalled to me the events that led him to discover for himself the truthfulness of the gospel and the Book of Mormon, or, in other terms, why he desired to serve a mission.

When working on the ranch, there would be times throughout the day when he would be driving a pickup truck loaded with different materials to the dump. Because there were other vehicles in line, my dad would pull out his copy of the Book of Mormon and read a few verses. On one specific occasion, he opened his scriptures and started to read. As he did so, he felt a spirit so strong within him that he thought his bones would melt. His eyes filled with tears as the Holy Ghost testified to him of the truthfulness of the

Book of Mormon. He vowed from that point on that he would serve the Lord, because he *knew* his confirmation came from Him.

He was called to serve in the Indiana-Michigan Mission in October 1971. He served faithfully under two mission presidents, but his last mission president would have a powerful impact on his life.

Because my dad held a leadership position in his mission, he worked at the mission home writing documents and assisting the president in other clerical duties. During holiday break, the president's children came home from their respective universities. This was the first time my father would see Stephanie Benson. She was a sophomore at Brigham Young University, studying piano performance. She had a bright countenance. Though my dad was strictly devoted to his missionary service, he felt a personal connection to this beautiful girl.

Upon returning from his mission in October 1973, my dad was pleasantly surprised to see that his father had returned to church activity. He still drank coffee every morning, but he had overcome his habits of smoking and drinking alcohol. My dad also thought about the beautiful young lady he met in the mission home that one holiday season and built up enough courage to ask her out. Through months of joy, some disappointments, and a lot of work, she would eventually accept his marriage proposal. My dad attributes his father's reactivity and his marriage to his eternal sweetheart to his decision to serve.

Now, this probably won't happen to everyone who serves a mission, but the point of this story is this:

You never know what your service will bring.

You never know the fruits that may come forth.

In the words of President Gordon B. Hinckley, "You never know how much good you do."[7]

Why serve? Because when you do, miracles happen. Hearts are changed, relationships are built, the Spirit is felt, and doors you thought were forever closed often lead to windows being opened for your benefit.

To conclude our discussion on the importance of understanding why we serve, I'd like to share a story from one of my favorite childhood Christmas movies.

During a scene in the film *Miracle on 34th Street,* Kris Kringle is gaining public acclaim due to his ability to present himself as a department store's Santa Claus; however, he is questioned because of his personal belief that he *is* Santa Claus. In response to one of these questioners, he explains, "I'm not just a whimsical figure who wears a charming suit and affects a jolly demeanor. You know, I'm a symbol. I'm a symbol of the human ability to be able to suppress the selfish and childish tendencies that rule a major part of our lives. If you can't believe, if you can't accept anything on faith, then you're doomed for a life dominated by doubt."[8]

Like the example of Santa Claus, a mission is a symbol. Service is a symbol. They are symbols of our love for the Lord. They are symbols of our desire to serve our brothers and sisters. They are, as Kris Kringle indicates, "A symbol of the human ability to be able to suppress the selfish and childish tendencies that rule . . . our lives."

I hope as we serve in our lives and within the Church, we will remember this counsel and choose to believe that what we are doing, no matter how small it may seem, is making a difference.

NOTES

1. Dallin H. Oaks, "Sharing the Restored Gospel," *Ensign*, Nov. 2016.
2. Sarah Jane Weaver, "Missionary Work Will Continue to Move Forward Despite COVID-19 Pandemic, Says Elder Uchtdorf," *Church News*, April 15, 2020. See churchofjesuschrist.org/church/news/. Accessed June 15, 2020.
3. Boyd K. Packer, "The Least of These," *Ensign*, Nov. 2004.
4. Thomas S. Monson, "Your Jericho Road," First Presidency Message, *Ensign*, Feb. 1989.
5. Dieter F. Uchtdorf, "Living the Gospel Joyful," *Ensign*, Nov. 2014.
6. Ibid., "Forget Me Not," *Ensign*, Nov. 2011.
7. Gordon B. Hinckley, "To the Women of the Church," *Ensign*, Nov. 2003.
8. *Miracle on 34th Street*, Twentieth Century Fox, produced by John Hughes and directed by Les Mayfield, 1994.

CHAPTER 2

SAYING GOODBYE

January 28, 2015. I had stayed up a little later the night before talking with my sisters about who knows what, trying to keep my mind off the inevitable journey that was to begin the following day. I remember going to bed with a mind that was surprisingly calm, yet I knew that when the alarm clock hit 6:30 a.m., my thoughts (and heart) would be racing like a Formula One car. I wish I could say I was 100 percent peaceful with my decision to serve a mission for The Church of Jesus Christ of Latter-day Saints and that the morning of my departure was going to be full of calmness, smiles, and laughter, but I'd be lying.

Though I knew in my heart that the decision I was making was the *right* one, it still didn't leave me without feelings of stress or anxiety.

That's something I wish more individuals knew about serving missions or making a decision that seems *right* in general. Yes, the Lord is proud of your decision, and yes, He is going to help you, but remember that His thoughts are higher than your thoughts, and His ways are higher than your ways. He may not leave you anxiety or stress free the morning your decision takes effect, but He will leave you with an underlying feeling of peace.

I arose on the morning of my scheduled departure with an anxiety I hadn't felt since I was a senior in high school getting ready to open the letter telling me if the application to the college of my choice was approved. I got dressed in my white shirt and tie, looked around my room for any last pictures or socks I had forgotten to pack, and zipped up my luggage. On my way downstairs, I smelled the pancakes my dad was preparing, something he had done every Saturday morning since I was a little kid. We ate, knelt for one final family prayer, and headed for the car. I remember looking at the house as we drove away. I whispered in my mind, *See you in two*. Little did I know that what I had thought would be two years was actually going to be two *months*.

As we got closer to the Missionary Training Center (MTC) in Provo, Utah, my mind raced at a more frantic pace. Who would my companions be? What would the language be like? Was I going to experience the soul-traumatizing anxiety I had felt as a young child going off to Scout camp? Could I do this?

STOP!

My self-talk caught hold of the questioning thoughts and threw them into a corner. Of course I could do this. Of course I was capable. The Lord had called me for a purpose. He would provide a way. I had been to a semester at college away from home. I had done hard things. I could do this mission.

We pulled into the parking lot, and I watched all the missionaries hugging their families goodbye.

Oh boy, I thought. *Okay, Drew, be strong. You can do this. You can do hard things.*

Little did I know then that those who struggle with mental illness or any emotional malady can't simply "gird up your loins" and "fresh courage take" with some self-talk and a pat on the back. You need more, and that's perfectly fine, but we'll get into that later in this book.[1]

My mom, dad, and brother walked me to the curb where another missionary greeted me with a smile. This was it. The moment I had been waiting and preparing for my entire life. I remembered my uncle recounting the day he had dropped his son, my cousin, off at the MTC. Instead of looking back and waving after hugging his family goodbye, his son walked in the doors with his head held high. I wanted to do the same. I gave my parents and brother a hug, grabbed my luggage, and didn't look back. I was really doing this.

NOTE

1. William Clayton, "Come, Come, Ye Saints," *Hymns*, no. 30 (Salt Lake City: The Church of Jesus Christ of Latter-day Saints, 1985).

CHAPTER 3

THE MISSIONARY TRAINING CENTER

A simple disclaimer before I talk about my experiences in the MTC: I am going to share personal and vulnerable things. Some are wonderful, and some are unpleasant. My purpose is not to tear down anyone or any process the Church has put into place. My intention is not to criticize the Provo MTC or any of the MTCs. It's not to shout, "Woe is me!" or make people lose their excitement of entering those sacred halls. I do not wish to blame, bash, or belittle anyone I speak of, whether they were teachers, leaders, or fellow missionaries. I made many fond, lifelong friends in the MTC and had many positive life-changing experiences. I will, however, speak the truth of what happened to me and what I experienced, hoping to help future individuals understand and perhaps prepare for their own experiences. I have never seen anything officially published from an actual missionary about what happens in the MTC. I hope to shed some light on that.

As anyone who has entered the MTC can attest, the first day (let alone the first week) is a roller-coaster ride of emotions. In fact, I remember one missionary saying to me, "If you can just get through the first week, you can make it through all of it."

You've just said goodbye to your family with the intention of not seeing them for a very long time—well not as long now since missionaries can call home every week, but that's a different story. You've said goodbye to friends and neighbors as you gave your farewell address. You're left with the expectations of miraculous baptisms, personal conversion, and life-changing experiences that will prepare you for anything and everything you will encounter after your mission is complete.

That wouldn't put an enormous amount of pressure on you at all, would it?

You pass through the front doors, your "companion," who picked you up on the curb, takes your luggage, and you enter the room where you receive a bag that has in it your ID card to get into all the buildings, a medical form, and, best of all, your missionary name tag. It is true when missionaries say that wearing the tag is like wearing a sacred mantle. Though the tag itself is just a piece of plastic, as we discussed in the first chapter, it is a symbol of a much higher and holier cause.

I put it on, and my identity changed from Drew Young to Elder Young, a *full-time* representative for the Savior of the world. It is truly an experience I will never forget.

You are then led to the bookstore where you get all the materials you will need for your stay. Your materials range in number from one to two or ten to twelve depending on what language you're speaking. For me, it was like going to the library at school to start studying for a hundred-page research paper. There were two vocabulary guides, a dictionary, a hymnbook (my personal favorite), a copy of the triple combination in Estonian, and a couple more things I can't remember.

Then, the part that every missionary anxiously anticipates, you go to the building where you will be introduced to your classroom and companions.

As we entered the building, we were led to a room of other missionaries who were in our "zone" but going to different missions. They had us fill out a questionnaire to make it easier for the branch presidency to get to know us better. One of the questions referred to mental illness and asked if the branch presidency needed to be aware of any issues we might have dealt with or were currently dealing with. I simply put that I had struggled with it in the past and that I would appreciate support and encouragement during my time at the MTC.

I then met my companions. A missionary is usually put with just one other member of the same gender, but I got two. How lucky I was . . . or maybe not. Now I didn't just have to be within "sight and sound" (an underlying rule of missionary companionships) of one person, but two at all times! One of my companions was from Missouri: quiet, reserved, teddy bear-like in nature, and easy to talk to. The other was from Wyoming: hardened exterior, red personality type, a hunter, and not afraid to speak his mind or be the center of attention. I still keep up with both and love them dearly, but from day one to day sixty-three, there would be many conflicts, companion inventories, and words I wish could be taken back because they were spoken to bluntly . . . but we'll get to that in a little bit. We also met the three sister missionaries who we would also be learning with every day. One was from Murray, Utah. She was also quiet, reserved, and easy to talk to. One was from Springville, Utah. She was an athlete who loved to sing, dance, and be happy. The third was from San Diego, California. She had already graduated from college, was very smart, and liked to stay on track with the lesson. I think God put the six of us together for a reason. Why? Because each of the three elders had a sister in the room who mirrored their personality.

We then walked down a brick hallway lined with classrooms. Within those classrooms, languages were being spoken that sounded like they were from other universes: Latvian, Malagasy, Greek, Georgian (not the US state). We got into our tiny room with barely enough space for six desks, where two teachers were there to greet us . . . in Estonian. And it wasn't just "Tere!" and "Nagamisani" (the words for "hello" and "goodbye" in Estonian), it was nonstop, no English, Estonian-only for a solid three hours. I thought my already overwhelmed brain was going to shut down. (Be prepared if you are learning a foreign language, because the teachers may not speak your native language to you.)

The rest of the night included dinner in the cafeteria, a welcome devotional, more Estonian instruction, and finally a meeting with our branch presidency who allowed us to handwrite one letter home to our parents letting them know we were still alive before we headed to our dorms for some much-needed rest.

That is how the first day at the MTC goes. Pretty interesting, right?

HARD TIMES

I would now like to transition from the structured first day experience to some of the hard times I experienced in the MTC. You may ask, "Why is Drew sharing hard things that happened in the MTC? He's just bitter he didn't get to serve the full two years and now he wants to tear the Church down any chance he gets. The MTC is a beautiful place and people are just doing the best they can. Stop pouting and get on with life."

This would be my response to someone who feels that way:

In recounting these experiences, I do not mean to demean or belittle any person or process set up by the Church or their leaders. I believe with all my heart that people genuinely have positive intentions at heart, regardless of how their actions come across. I cherish my experiences in the MTC. They have shaped me more profoundly than almost any other experiences I've ever had. I share because I care. I share because some people out there are like me: sensitive (maybe too sensitive at times), trying to do their best, but who may struggle with illnesses or conditions (dyslexia, hyper-sensitivity, perfectionism, anxiety, depression, OCD, ADHD, ADD, and so on) that aren't fully recognized or understood by a lot of people, no matter how legitimate they may be. I share because perhaps my experience will help those reading this feel like they are understood and heard.

"Obedience brings blessings, but exact obedience brings miracles."

On the first night that the entire zone met with the branch presidency, we were introduced to what is called the "7-7-7 rule." This was supposed to hold each missionary accountable for his or her actions throughout the week when it came to waking up each day at 6:30 a.m., being in their own rooms by 10:15 p.m. for quiet time, and then having lights out by 10:30 p.m. We were then to email a member of the branch presidency every preparation day and report on our obedience to the 7-7-7 rule.

Looking back, I can see that this rule was most likely put into place to give each missionary a yardstick to measure his or her obedience by, but for me, it "woke me up" to how inadequate and imperfect of a missionary I was. Each preparation day I would be down on my knees in tears pleading for forgiveness because I had gotten up at 6:32 a.m. one morning or had gone to bed at 10:40 p.m. because I was up empathizing with another missionary and trying to offer him comfort.

In my mind, I thought, *How is the Lord supposed to bless me if I have a 6-5-5 for the week? How can I learn the language if I am not exactly obedient?*

One week I just wasn't my best. I had been struggling for a month with anxiety, had trouble sleeping, and the ten- to twelve-hour classroom days with only thirty minutes of time outside was crippling me. I wrote a member of my branch presidency, "It's been a really hard week for me. I'm just struggling. This week I had 4-5-5. I'm sorry."

He responded something to the effect, "Elder Young, thanks for telling me, but c'mon, that's not good enough and I know you can do better."

I read it and wept.

"That's the problem," I whispered. "I *can't* do better. No matter how hard I try, this illness prevents me from *doing* better. I am never going to be the *perfect* missionary that everyone expects me to be. I am a failure. How can the Lord bless me for this?"

I know, it sounds crazy and dramatic, right? But it's true! This is exactly how I felt, and it's exactly what happened. I wasn't the only missionary who was feeling this way. Many missionaries were haunted by the phrase that floated around the MTC and mission field, "Obedience brings blessings, but *exact* obedience brings miracles."

Just for a moment, let's drop the missionary title and apply this phrase to the Church's culture as a whole. I know countless people (young adults, college students, missionaries, and senior citizens) who have either left the Church or gone inactive because of the expectations, real or imagined, that are placed on them.

Expectations are not bad, but false expectations are.

Sometimes we are so caught up with the expectation of perfection in the here and now that we lose sight of what really matters: growth.

That's what the Lord cares about. Not speed, but direction. He didn't say, "Come, run to me and do it as fast as you can, with complete exactness so everyone can see how perfect you are."

He said, "Come, follow me."

In my mind, what the Savior means is this, "When you follow me, that doesn't just mean you walk behind me blindly like I'm some drill sergeant. What I want is for you to *focus* on me. *Watch* me. *Yoke* yourself to me. Don't worry about what the other kids in school are doing. Don't concern yourself with your companion's weaknesses or your spouse's sins. Just follow me. And when you mess up, repent and come back. I'm here for you."

We need to teach our children this. We need to teach it again, and again, and again. We need to teach it in the MTCs. We need to teach it in priesthood and Relief Society groups. We have been taught to think we are not enough because we make mistakes and numbers determine our worth: how many times we read our scriptures, how many times we pray, how many times we go to Church, and so on. Our spiritual stature and identity are not determined by how many times we get up at 6:30 a.m. or go to bed at exactly 10:30 p.m. (insert your own narrative). They are measured by how we choose to follow Christ and how loyal we are to Him, because most people who follow Christ in faith and love don't all fit into the same mold.

We don't read our scriptures, pray, serve, go to Church, or go on missions because they will get us into heaven. We do those things because they teach us of Christ, and as we come unto Christ, *we will want to be like Him and live with Him.* It's all about Him. He needs to be our focus.

So, what can we do?

Here's what we can do, and this is all life asks of us:

We can make measurable progress in reasonable time.

We can grow.

We can choose to follow the Savior a little better today than we did yesterday, and that is enough.

"I was just seeing how far I could go."

I had three wonderful teachers during my stay at the MTC. Each was different from the other, but they all had a profound impact on me. There were, however, some rocky times. One day, early in the MTC experience, we were in the first of our four three-hour blocks of learning for the day. These typically consisted of vocabulary, preparing for/teaching our investigators, going through *Preach My Gospel* and other activities.

As one could guess, this can become exhausting. I felt I needed more frequent breaks than I received to refresh and come back prepared to learn more. The teacher seemed to be unaware that I couldn't handle more content and could have used a break.

As the lesson progressed from 60 to 90 to 120 minutes, I, and the rest of our group, were becoming emotionally drained. My mind was so full and exhausted that I couldn't take anymore. We hadn't had any breaks longer than two minutes (though we asked multiple times), and I didn't understand a single word of what was being said. Finally, after 180 minutes of nonstop teaching, they concluded their lesson. We knelt to say a prayer, and I began to sob. The other missionaries looked up at me, wondering what the matter was. As the prayer concluded, I slowly got up, put my dictionary and vocabulary journal back into my desk, and headed for the door.

The teacher noticed how emotional I was and started to talk to me . . . in Estonian.

Let me repeat, I had just had 180 nonstop minutes of Estonian shoved into my brain, and now when all I needed was someone to speak something understandable to me, I heard more Estonian.

Now, before I go on with the remainder of the story, let me make something clear. I do not blame the teacher for what happened. I know her intentions were pure. Sure, if I was in Estonia on the streets, probably no one would approach me and comfort me in the English language . . . but that's just it. I wasn't in Estonia yet. It's not called the Estonian (or Spanish, Russian, or French) Language Training Center. It's called the Missionary Training Center.

I have no idea what my teacher said when she started talking to me in Eastonian. After seeing me unable to communicate my feelings effectively, she finally spoke English and asked, "What's wrong. Are you all right?"

"No," I responded. "I guess I'm just a little overwhelmed with how exhausting that lesson was."

Then came the line that hurt me the most.

"Oh, Elder Young. I just wanted to see how far I could go."

I was baffled. I left that exchange wondering, *How many other members of the Church are feeling misunderstood, overwhelmed, and at the mercy of those who are "just seeing how far they can go" in teaching the gospel and setting expectations?*

That is what I experienced for sixty-three days in the MTC and many days after. That is what many missionaries and members alike experience within this Church: teachers, leaders, and parents that don't know what to look for or how to handle an individual that, although happy and cheerful on the outside, is dealing with a tornado of anxiety, fear, and distress on the inside.

And that is why I wrote this book. That is why I am speaking out. Not to condemn anyone, but to help young adults, parents, teachers, and friends understand that there is a need for this. There is a need for everyone to realize that just because you can't see someone in a cast, it doesn't mean they are without injury (emotional or physical). Now, that doesn't mean that we need to develop an ulcer due to worrying about whether we are saying the right things all the time; but it does mean that now is the time for everyone to come together, be kind, empathize with one another, and see others for who they can become.

GREAT TIMES

Now, on to the times that brought me indescribable joy. The MTC is a place where the Spirit of Christ is strong. Unlike most times/places in life, you can know that at almost any time of the day or night, there is someone in the world praying for you. You are on almost every temple prayer roll, you're being fasted for, and many people are pulling for you.

The Character of Christ

The amazing part about the MTC is that it is a spiritual feast. There's probably more praying, scripture reading, testimony sharing, and hymn singing in a given hour than anywhere else in the world.

When I first arrived, I was told that every six weeks a member of the Quorum of the Twelve Apostles would come to do a devotional. I would be there for nine, so my heart jumped with excitement when I heard. Because the missionaries never learned who would be speaking until the night of, each Sunday was a surprise. I remember looking forward to hearing the messages of encouragement, love, and hope from various ecclesiastical leaders.

One Sunday we didn't have a speaker come, so we could either watch the movie *Meet the Mormons* or go to the auditorium to watch a past devotional given by Elder David A. Bednar titled, *The Character of Christ*. My companions and I went to watch the devotional, and it was one of the most spiritual experiences of my life.

For those who are unfamiliar with this talk, it was given at BYU–Idaho in the early 2000s but re-given at the MTC one Christmas. The basis of the talk surrounds two principles: first, the reality that whenever Christ was in a position where most people would turn inward to satisfy their own needs, He would turn outward to help someone else. Second, in order for Christ to be who He was, His character had to be perfect, and the only way His character could be made perfect would be through overcoming temptation and trial. Elder Bednar related a story in the Savior's life that demonstrated this principle in pristine fashion.

> The New Testament is replete with "strikingly displayed" examples of the Savior's character. We are all well aware that following His baptism by John the Baptist and as a preparation for His public ministry, the Savior fasted for forty days. He also was tempted by the adversary to inappropriately use His supernal power to satisfy physical desires by commanding that stones be made bread, to gain recognition by casting Himself down from the pinnacle of the temple, and to obtain wealth and power and prestige in exchange for falling down and worshiping the tempter (see Matthew 4:1–9). It is interesting to note that the overarching and fundamental challenge to the Savior in each of these three temptations is contained in the taunting statement, *"If thou be the Son of God."* Satan's strategy, in essence, was to dare the Son of God to improperly demonstrate His God-given powers, to sacrifice meekness and modesty, and, thereby, betray who He was. Thus, Satan attempted repeatedly to attack Jesus's understanding of who He was and of His relationship with His Father. Jesus was victorious in meeting and overcoming the strategy of Satan.[1]

Elder Bednar continued to explain that when the devil left the Savior after failing to get him to succumb to temptation, angels came and ministered to Him. However, there is a translation, the Joseph Smith Translation (JST), that adds extra meaning to what this meant. Yes, Jesus would have benefitted greatly from ministering angels, but the JST clearly states that after the devil left him, Jesus remembered that John was suffering in prison, so He sent the angels to minister to him instead. How interesting, how beautiful, how humbling it is for us to realize that when Christ was amid his own temptation and trial, he sent angels to someone else, clearly indicating his divine character in turning outward when the natural man would have turned inward.

As I listened to this message, tears welled up in my eyes. Here I was, going through my own trials, emotionally distraught and physically exhausted, and the Lord was standing next to me saying, "Don't worry. I've got your back. I am here for you. My character wouldn't allow me to give you anything less than my absolute best."

It was comforting to know that I had a Savior who had overcome hardship, temptation, and turmoil, and that I could too with his help.

The MTC was full of spiritually life-altering experiences that left me in awe of the Savior's love and power, but in no greater capacity did I feel the Savior's love than when I sat and listened to messages given by His servants.

Songs of Glory unto Thee

President J. Reuben Clark Jr. once said, "We get nearer to the Lord through music than perhaps through any other thing except prayer."[2]

The Spirit of Christ is profoundly evident in hymns that speak, testify, and glory in His name. The MTC has no shortage of opportunities to sing, but I would like to share two personal experiences.

The first occasion came when I was blessed with the chance to sing in the missionary choir. Every Sunday for an hour, a missionary could leave their current companion(s) if they wanted to join another missionary at choir practice.

I thought this would be a good opportunity to clear my head, relieve some stress, and meet more missionaries. As we gathered in the auditorium, the conductor told us that we were going to sing *Consider the Lilies,* a beautiful hymn that testifies of Christ's concern over all His creations. The song is a testament that He cares about each one of us no matter how "small" we think we are.

I gained a strong appreciation for the power of singing as we practiced. I would take what I learned in practice and apply it throughout the week. Whether I was in the shower, walking between class and lunch, or doing laundry on preparation day, I sang every chance I could. It was my home away from home, and my biggest stress reliever. Though I enjoyed it profusely, my companions can attest that I made them red in the face at times because of the volume (and probably pitch) of my singing.

The second occasion came when I had the opportunity to learn about the story of Joseph Smith's First Vision in the *Pearl of Great Price*. As one would guess, memorizing the First Vision in any language other than your native tongue would be a challenge, but for me, learning it in Estonian was nearly impossible. I tried to say each word, looking at an Estonian-English dictionary for the definition, and then continuing in the sentence. Doing this took hours to get through just one paragraph, and I was forgetting more than I was remembering.

Then one day as I was in the temple, reading through the First Vision in English, I had a thought come to my mind. *Drew, why not memorize the First Vision by singing it?*

At first I was caught off guard by the idea. I had never memorized anything in my life by putting it to a tune and singing it. But the fact that the thought came to me while I was in the temple (where the veil between heaven and earth is thin) and that I was determined to learn the language and the lessons any way I could, propelled me to put it into practice.

I got back to the classroom, opened my Estonian copy of the *Restoration* pamphlet, and started singing the words to the tune, "Joseph Smith's First Prayer."[3] To my astonishment, I would remember what I sang far better than when I just said it out loud. I'm sure this wasn't fun for missionaries listening in surrounding classrooms (bless their hearts . . . and ears), but by the end of that week, I had memorized the entire First Vision in Estonian.

Singing not only relieved my stress and built my testimony of Christ, but it also gave me a better way to memorize the language that the Lord wanted me to learn. Five years later, there isn't a day that goes by that I don't sing. It doesn't matter if it's hymns or just feel-good music on Spotify. Whether it's in the car, in the shower, or just getting ready for the day, it still relieves my stress, brings joy into my life, and helps me deal more effectively with any problems I may be facing.

LESSONS LEARNED

First, go to the temple.

It's a holy place. It's a place of refuge and peace. It's a place to get away from the bullies, exams, stresses, deadlines, and problems of life. If you don't have a temple recommend, just go to the temple grounds. The Lord will bless you for your effort to be near Him and His house.

Second, don't be afraid to try something different, even if it's something you have not done in the past.

If I had never gone to that choir practice, I wouldn't have been introduced to the power of singing, which led me to sing more often in everyday life and helped me accomplish my goal of learning the language and gaining a stronger testimony of Christ.

What's your "First Vision" that you need to "memorize"? What's your goal that you are trying to accomplish? Think outside the box, and if you get an unorthodox thought while doing so, follow it. It just might be the thing that helps you accomplish your goal, no matter how crazy it seems.

Notes

1. David A. Bednar, "A Christlike Character," Brigham Young University–Idaho Religion Symposium address, January 25, 2003.
2. J. Reuben Clark, in Conference Report, Oct. 1936, 111.
3. *Hymns*, no. 26.

CHAPTER 4

COMING HOME

March 30, 2015. The past sixty-three days had been a roller coaster of ups and downs, twists and turns, and it all lead me to this place.

Backstory: A few weeks prior to this day, I had visited with a therapist at the MTC that I saw once a week to check on my progress. The first few weeks she assumed I was like many of the missionaries who came to see her: homesick and discouraged but would pull through. I wasn't that missionary.

SIDE NOTE—Therapy can be life changing, and everyone should try it regardless of his or her personal circumstances. Seriously, get over your pride and bias and go see or call a therapist. It may be the greatest thing you've ever done.

It was our third week of meeting, and as I was explaining to her how debilitating my anxiety had become (I couldn't sleep, I was gaining an unhealthy amount of weight, and I was having panic attacks on almost an hourly basis), she leaned in and said to me, "Elder Young, I was wrong. I thought this was just another case of homesickness, but it's not, is it?"

I responded with my head down, "No. I want to be here so badly. I want to serve the Lord . . . I just can't."

That's the thing with mental or emotional fatigue. It isn't just a "those who motivate themselves get through it" type of thing. It's hard, it's debilitating, and it's *real*.

She then said, "I'm finally realizing that you're on the Titanic, and you're going down fast."

It's hard to write the feelings associated with the moment when those words were said. It was as if my heart was saying, "Yes! Get me out of here. I can't do this anymore! Finally, someone understands the pain I'm experiencing. Please, please, just get me out of here so I can start feeling some relief!"

But the feelings in my Spirit were coming from a completely different place: "No! Please don't say I have to go home. I want to be here. I want to serve. I want to accomplish the mission the Lord has given me. Tell me how I can get through this."

Matthew 26:41 never made more sense to me then at that time. "Truly, the Spirit is willing, but the flesh is weak."

The therapist decided to take my case to the MTC medical committee, where they evaluated my psychiatric progress. My therapist met with the head doctor, as well as a few of the district presidents in the MTC. After deliberation, they came to the consensus that I was "fit for missionary service."

A few weeks had gone by after that visit. I had been introduced to the MTC doctor, been prescribed medicine for the first time in my life, was still seeing my therapist every week, and was trying to adapt myself to the emotional and mental changes the medicine was making in me.

There were days when I would try new medication (I tried about three different types in five weeks), feel completely like my old self again, but would then hit a wall when my brain would end up rejecting the medicine, making me more depressed than ever before.

Then came week nine, the last week before my entire zone was to be shipped out to their respective missions. As my therapist and I sat down for our final visit, our conversation became more serious than ever before. The past few weeks had been difficult, and I wasn't making as much emotional and psychological progress as she wanted to see. I was still fighting debilitating discouragement, experiencing panic attacks on almost a daily basis, and as far as she could tell, there was not a light at the end of the tunnel.

I knew it too. What would I do if I had an anxiety attack on the airplane? What if everyone saw me crying in the airport, not because I was homesick, but because I was *ill*? What if I needed medication in Estonia and there wasn't a doctor I could go see that knew me personally? These questions weighed on my mind.

The therapist made the decision to take my psychiatric situation before the medical committee one more time.

It was a Saturday night, just two days before we were to leave for Estonia. My bags were packed and weighed, and my companions and I were sitting at dinner in the cafeteria. I received a message informing me to go to one of the district president's offices. My companions gave me a look of encouragement as I got up and made my way past the enormous map that every missionary takes a picture of as they point to their respective missions. Into my mind came the thought, "I wonder if Estonia *is* my mission?"

This thought would end up coming back to my mind many times throughout the next several months and years.

As I got into the president's office, he greeted me, closed the door, and calmly said,

"Elder Young, we've (the medical committee) reviewed your progress the past few weeks, have spoken with your therapist and mission president, and have come to the conclusion that you should return home, get better, and see if you can come back out in a couple months."

My minded started racing with different questions. *What would my parents think? What would my friends think? Why me?*

Then I was filled with a sense of hope I hadn't experienced my entire time at the MTC. I was actually going to be able to heal. I didn't have to worry about having every single day filled with almost incalculable stress and expectation. This could be good!

The district president then invited me to get on the phone and call my parents. They were going to have to come to the MTC the next day to pick me up. As I dialed the number, my hands began to shake.

What will my family think? Will they think I failed? What will my dad think?

My dad and I had always talked about me serving a mission like he and my three older brothers had. All of them were assistants to their mission presidents, had life-changing experiences on their missions, and had *completed* their missions—no matter what challenges they experienced. I was about to break that expectation. I was about to show my dad that I couldn't beat this challenge and accomplish my mission. I'm sure many of you reading this have had similar experiences in your own life, regardless of what circumstances you were under.

SIDE NOTE—I did end up beating the challenge and accomplishing *my* Latter-day Saint mission, but it wasn't the mission I had expected or desired. It was the mission the Lord had in store for me. That's the thing about missions, as much as we make them out to be about *us* and *our* experiences, they really are and should be about the Lord. It is the Lord's mission, and we are just instruments in His hands to accomplish His purposes.

Never in my entire life have I wanted to let my dad down, but it was in those next thirty seconds that I have never ever felt like I let someone down as much in my life.

"Hi dad."

"Hi, Andrew. What's up?"

"So, the medical committee has just told me they think it's best if I come home for the next couple months so I can get better."

Five seconds of dead air that felt like five minutes.

"Well, all right then. We'll see you tomorrow."

That was the conversation. I handed the phone over to the district president to finish the phone call, and I headed back to the cafeteria. To anyone who may think that my dad was cold or unsympathetic—don't judge him. You don't know my dad's heart. He is my hero, and we have a great relationship to this day.

The next day I told the remainder of the missionaries in my zone that I was going home, ending each conversation with, "But don't worry. It's just for a couple of months, and I'll be back out."

Again, I misunderstood the fact that it wasn't my mission and timing. It was the Lord's.

That evening, my companions and I were gathered around the common area in our building when the phone rang.

"Hi, Elder Young. This is the front desk. Your family has just arrived to pick you up. Please come to the front office."

I grabbed my luggage, put on my suit coat, and headed for the front office. My companions, as well as the sisters in my district, joined me. As we got closer and closer, there wasn't much conversation going on. I think everyone was emotionally spent from the past nine weeks.

We walked through the front doors and I saw my family. I didn't know whether to smile or to cry. This wasn't how missionaries were supposed to return home. No banners, no signs, no balloons, no "Welcome Home Elder"—certainly not after only sixty-three days. I gave my parents a soft hug and my brothers as well. It was as awkward a situation as I've ever had. I didn't want to speak to anyone. I didn't want anyone to see me. I just wanted to be alone.

I said goodbye to my companions, walked out to the car, and we drove to the stake center to meet the stake president.

He welcomed me into his office, sat me down, and told me a few things that I don't remember—except one. As we concluded the conversation, he looked me in the eyes and said, "Now Elder Young, this is just a temporary detour, but because you are no longer a missionary, I need you to take your name tag off."

For ten seconds I sat in hesitation. I thought, *I've only been a missionary for sixty-three days. I've let my family down, and now I've let the Lord down. How could I take off the only thing that's given me a sense of comfort and purpose the last nine weeks?*

He looked at me again and nodded his head.

I slowly took my name tag off, slipped it into my suit coat pocket, and dropped my head. I had failed.

CHAPTER 5

NOW WHAT?
COMING TO GRIPS WITH REALITY

I remember pulling into the driveway, getting out of the car, grabbing my luggage, and seeing a familiar car from a friend's house pass in front of our house. A wave of guilt and embarrassment passed over me. I wanted to disappear.

I went to bed that night in tears, questioning myself constantly. *Did I do the right thing? Is my mission over? Will I ever get better enough to go back out? How do my parents really feel about the fact that I've come home early?*

Have you ever had an experience in your life that made you question if the decision you made was the right one? Has something ever happened to you that went against the status quo, even if it wasn't your fault, and you felt like your life was never going to be the same?

The next day, my dad had me working in the yard, trying to keep my mind away from negative thoughts by staying busy. As I was pulling weeds by the front door, neighbors pulled into their driveway across the street. Trying not to act completely awkward, I stood up and waved. They waved back, though their faces looked puzzled. I could only imagine what they were thinking,

"Why is Elder Young home? I wonder what he did. . . . Oh gosh, I don't want him to feel awkward. Let's just wave, go inside, and tell the rest of our family."

As crazy as this may seem, just the next day, without my knowledge at the time, another neighbor tweeted about my arrival home, making fun of the fact that I had come home early while his best friend who was only a recent convert was still on his mission.

As one could only guess, this made my transition from "mission life" to "civilian life" more traumatic. Not only did I have to deal with a sickness that was new territory, but I also felt as if people were watching me and every move I made.

I once heard a profound leadership executive say, "A organization's culture is the only thing that can't be duplicated, and gossip is the metaphorical cancer of any organization's culture."

Gossip is the metaphorical cancer of The Church of Jesus Christ of Latter-day Saints.

When we talk behind other people's backs, no matter how pure our intentions may be, we run the risk of spreading rumors that aren't fully true, and that can cause severe damage. We also hurt our own personal brand. If I'm talking with Stacy or Tom, and they are gossiping about one of our neighbors, I know I'm next. Gossipers are no respecter of persons. They don't care who they gossip about. They just care about being noticed and having attention. So, when tempted to gossip about someone, remember this:

We don't have all the facts.

We don't know why something has happened, or why someone is the way they are.

On the other hand, defending those who are absent can create a culture of trust and love. As Stephen R. Covey once said, "When you defend those who are absent, you retain the trust of those present."[1]

The Church of Jesus Christ of Latter-Day Saints prides itself on and is known globally for the love we show people of every culture and creed. We are of the first responders in any worldwide natural disaster, and our donations help pay for food, water, wheelchairs, and medical treatments for millions in need. Let us make it a goal as friends, neighbors, and a church to focus a little less on the "behind-the-scenes" of other people's lives and focus a more on how we can help, lift, and strengthen those in need.

Though these experiences were difficult for me to cope with, I discovered three principles that helped me to persevere, slowly heal, and focus on my relationship with Christ more than anything else. I would recommend them to anyone struggling with a gospel-related or emotional issue:

1. Staying Active
2. Making Investments
3. Seeking Professional Help

SIDE NOTE—In recounting any of these personal stories, I do not mean to say that there are only three correct ways to do something when you're dealing with an issue. So, my advice would be for you to be a student, not a follower. Don't just follow blindly what I say, but find out for yourself and try it for two weeks. If it works, keep it. If it doesn't work, change it.

NOTE

1. Stephen R. Covey, *The 7 Habits of Highly Effective People* (New York: Free Press, 1989), 196.

CHAPTER 6

THREE PILLARS OF PEACE

STAYING ACTIVE

I'll never forget my first Sunday back. That entire first week I experienced an identity crisis like never before. There wasn't a day go by that I didn't think to myself, *Who am I? What will my future look like? Why do my family and friends keep asking me when I'll go back on my mission when I haven't even had time to figure out my future? Is there something wrong with me?*

I'd had the whole week to lie low, but this would be the first time I would be seen by *everyone* in the ward, and I was terrified. I remember getting ready for church in my oversized suit that I was supposed to "grow into" over the next two years and wondering to myself how I was going to tell everyone what happened to me and what my future was.

As crazy as this may seem, I even considered walking into church with some crutches so that people wouldn't automatically judge me. It wouldn't have been a bad idea, since people judge what is on the outside (1 Samuel 16:7), and discouragement, anxiety, and shame are often hidden underneath a guise of smiling and laughter.

I have, of course, learned since that day that you don't have to explain anything to anyone. Nor do you need to justify anything regarding mental illness, discouragement, or heartache. They are real, and they are legitimate. Remember that what other people think about you is none of your business. Be yourself, be good, and be steadfast. Let other people spend their time and emotional energy on judging, teasing, and gossiping.

As we entered the chapel, it was as if a spotlight turned on. I felt that all eyes were on me. The entire day was filled with members asking me all types of questions that were tough to answer, not because they were hard, but because I didn't know the answers myself.

I went home feeling like crawling under my bed and spending the rest of my life there. No one understood me. No one knew what I had been through. No one could even *see* my illness. I never wanted to go to church again.

It ended up being a difficult first month back since each Sunday more and more people would approach me and ask me questions. I had to make up a time line for when I would return. I felt I wasn't good enough. I felt my testimony slipping and my desire to give up growing.

It was at this point that I learned something life-changing. People don't stop coming to Church because of broken covenants or commandments. They stop coming because of *man-made* judgments and expectations. Though spoken with good intentions, these man-made expectations and judgments make them feel they can never measure up. We need to change that.

Then I heard a story that changed my perspective and helped me commit to focusing on Christ instead of everyone else. Perhaps it can help you too.

A lady went to her [bishop] and said, "[Bishop], I won't be going to your church anymore."

He responded, "But why?"

The lady said, "Ah! I saw a woman gossiping about another member; a man that is a hypocrite; the [relief society] living wrong; people looking at their phone during [sacrament] service; among so many other things wrong in your church."

The [bishop] replied, "Okay, but before you go, do me a favor: take a full glass of water and walk around the church three times without spilling a drop on the ground. Afterward, leave the church if you desire."

The lady thought, *Too easy!* She walked three times around the church as the [bishop] had asked. When she finished, she told the [bishop] she was ready to leave.

He said, "Before you leave, I want to ask you one more question. When you were walking around the church, did you see anyone gossiping?"

The lady replied, "No."

"Did you see any hypocrites?"

The lady said, "No."

"Anyone looking at their phone?"

"No."

"You know why?"

"No."

"You were focused on the glass to make sure you didn't stumble and spill any water."

It's the same with our lives. When we keep our eyes on Jesus, we don't have time to see the mistakes of others. We will reach out a helping hand to them and concentrate on our own walk with the Lord.[1]

Two lessons here: First, regardless of whether it's church, school, work, or relationships, you get out what you put in. If you give half effort, the result will be half as good as it could've been. If you give full effort, even if the result isn't what you expected, you won't have to worry, because you gave it your all. Second, once you think the problem has nothing to do with you, that is the problem. Once you start blaming everything and everyone else for your problems, you make your situation inevitably worse. The problem isn't your best friend. The problem isn't your parents. The problem isn't your ward, your work, or your school. The problem is how you *view* and *deal* with those things.

If you become bitter, life will be bitter. If you gossip and bully others around, your relationships will be shallow and fleeting. On the other hand, if you are grateful and kind, life will reciprocate. If you are abundant-minded and generous, life will show the same to you. That doesn't mean you wear rose-colored glasses and think everything is great all the time. It does mean that you *choose* to think the best of everyone and decide that you are going to make it regardless of your circumstances. As an old leader of mine used to say, "If it's to be, it's up to me!"

This was my problem. I was focused on the wrong thing. I was focused on what other people thought of me. I was focused on blaming everyone else (family, ward members, and God) for my problems. I was focused on what was wrong with my circumstances instead of trying to make something good out of them. I was blaming everyone else *besides* myself. I used to sit in my room or in church and complain to God, "Why?! Why me?! Why now?! I don't deserve this!"

Half a decade later, I realize I should've had the mindset of, "Why *not?* Why *not* me? Why *not* now? I can do hard things. I can make smart decisions. I can turn nothing into something. I can make a disappointment into an appointment. I am in control of my future!"

I cannot tell you the definitive secret to success in life, but I can tell you three things that create failure in life almost 100 percent of the time:

Trying to please everyone.

Trying to blame everyone.

Not taking responsibility for your actions.

If we are focused only on the flaws and the imperfections of ourselves or someone else, we will easily find them, but if we are focused solely on doing the best we can with what we have and where we are, the distractions will fade away.

When I started taking responsibility for how my life turned out and started focusing exclusively on Christ, my testimony gradually strengthened and the clouds of fear and anxiety began to lift. That doesn't mean I still didn't have moments of "I'm never going to be good enough" or feel that I was being misunderstood or falsely judged. What it does mean is that I found someone and something I could rely on. I found someone who understood me when no one else had a clue what I was going through.

Christ understands mental illness.

Christ understands discouragement.

Christ understands heartache.

Christ understands YOU.

He will lighten the load of all those who come unto Him (Moroni 10:32).

As time progressed, things got easier, not because the trial had lessened, but because my capacity to endure had strengthened. As Ralph Waldo Emerson so poetically wrote, "That which we persist in doing becomes easier for us to do—not that the nature of the thing has changed, but that our power to do has increased."[2]

I learned that God doesn't want us to go to church just for the people there, though it can certainly make a difference. He wants us to go to church because that is where we learn more of Christ, and it is through Christ that we receive "life more abundantly" (John 10:10).

For those who may be doubting the Church or their testimonies, I have one piece of advice: stay active.

It can be hard, I know. But it's worth it. Even if some things are said that sting, members have the best of intentions in their hearts. Even if you feel pressured at times, the bishopric, relief society, and priesthood quorums just want you to feel welcome. Take a deep breath and realize no one is perfect. The storms will pass. Forgive and you will be forgiven. The test will turn into a testimony, and the trial will turn into a triumph. I don't know how long it will take, but I do know that if you hold on, trust on, and put one foot in front of the other, you will make it. Don't give in and don't give up. Believe in yourself and believe in Him.

MAKING INVESTMENTS

The dictionary denotes the term *sacrifice* as an act of giving up something valued for the sake of something else regarded as more important or worthy.

When it comes to The Church of Jesus Christ of Latter-day Saints, we speak a lot about sacrifice. One of the most popular hymns from the Restoration declares, "Sacrifice brings forth the blessings of heaven."[3] Talks have been given in sacrament meetings and general conferences about the rewards of sacrifice with our time and actions.

I believe that a lot of people associate sacrifice as something that is inevitably hard or difficult, a metaphorical "thorn in the side" (2 Corinthians 12:7) and don't pay attention to the part following the sacrifice where they experience something of much greater value. Perhaps the cultural beliefs surrounding sacrifice stem from the pioneers and how they literally had to sacrifice *everything* to make a new life for themselves, some even dying in the process. Brigham Young couldn't say, "Go and do the best you can, and you'll be blessed, regardless of the outcome." He had to say, "You must go. You must persevere. You must push through, even until death. Excuses are unacceptable."

Though our current generation owes most (if not all) of where we are at as a Church to the beloved pioneers, to compare a sacrifice in this day and age to what the pioneers went through in their individual circumstances would not be accurate. I am not discounting the pioneers for what they had to go through. I am not downplaying the sacrifices they made. In their specific circumstances they had to persevere or die, and if they didn't physically, emotionally, and spiritually exhaust themselves, they would not have made it. They are heroes.

But we aren't pioneers. We aren't supposed to have the mindset of "persevere or die." We aren't supposed to physically, emotionally, and spiritually exhaust ourselves to prove a point or attain a result.

So, what are we to do in our modern day? What are we to do when it comes to sacrifice in our lives without "killing" ourselves? Perhaps changing our paradigms by altering our perspective may help some who are struggling with these questions.

The term *investment* is defined as "an act of devoting time, effort, or energy to a particular undertaking with the expectation of a worthwhile result."

I prefer to simply change the current perspective of sacrifice and turn it into investment. Whenever most people hear the term investment, they don't automatically think of something bad/hard/more-cons-than-pros. They think of something that requires work and time, which has the potential to yield a far greater reward than the initial effort put in. I don't think Heavenly Father intended us to become discouraged when hearing that we would have to sacrifice some things for others. I think He wanted us to look beyond the initial *loss* to a far greater *return*. In addition, I believe He wants us to, as the definition explains, *expect* a worthwhile result. He wants us to expect happiness, energy, forgiveness, and joy when we do what He asks. He is good. He is our Father. We need to trust in His love for us and the fact that because He loves us, He needs to, at times, put us through difficult things that in the moment hurt but will eventually yield far greater results.

Some may abuse that saying and simply follow the commandments because they want blessings, but we all know that doesn't provide lasting conversion. We follow Him because we love Him, and in the process of doing so, we are guided and strengthened.

With that introduction, I have chosen four investments that, if followed and pursued diligently, will make life more peaceful and bring one closer to their Heavenly Father and Savior Jesus Christ.

They are

1. Prayer
2. Scripture Study
3. Temple Attendance
4. Service to Others

Prayer

Abraham Lincoln once said, "I have been driven many times upon my knees by the overwhelming conviction that I had nowhere else to go."[4]

Prayer is a safe haven. When we pray to our Heavenly Father in the name of Jesus Christ, we are promised that we are heard, blessed, and guided

(James 1:5–6). Even if we may feel like there is a "mute button" on our prayers and they are not being heard on the other side, I have no doubt that God knows our hearts perfectly. He answers in His own way and in His own time, but by praying we *immediately* fill the hole this world leaves in our souls.

In addition, listening is a key ingredient in praying. When we listen, we allow the veil between heaven and us to become very thin.

As I spent the first month at home, I felt constantly attacked by the adversary. Every weapon of his was thrown at me: temptations to fall back into old negative habits, feelings of worthlessness and unworthiness, a constant pressure to retreat from prayer and scripture study, and so on. Some of you may be experiencing those same attacks. Regardless of your personal circumstances, prayer will help.

One night, when I was almost ready to throw in the "spiritual" towel, I offered one of the sincerest prayers of my life. He answered. Even if it wasn't on my timetable, looking back it was perfect timing. I received confirmation that I was doing the right thing. I was where He needed me. This came after *many* long days and nights of loneliness, fear, and feeling like I was forgotten.

It seems like everything that truly matters in this life takes time.

Days, weeks, months, or even years may be required, but the result of our patience and our prayers will yield profound peace.

I invite you to pray and ask God how He feels about you. Ask Him if you're in the right place in your life, and then listen and be ready to hear His voice.

Scripture Study

President Spencer W. Kimball explained,

> I find that when I get casual in my relationships with divinity and when it seems that no divine ear is listening, and no divine voice is speaking, that I am far, far away. If I immerse myself in the scriptures the distance narrows and the spirituality returns.[5]

Imagine for a minute that your dearest friends and family members from hundreds of years ago had seen you in a dream, knew of your life, your strengths and fears, and had written you letters of encouragement, counsel, and love that were specifically designed to help you with the problems you would face. Imagine them running through forests and deserts to preserve those letters for you, some even giving their lives so that their message would make it to you. Now imagine those letters sitting on your nightstand. Would you read them?

I'm sure that many of us, if not all, would exclaim with an emphatic, "*Yes!*"

Well, these letters are what the scriptures are. It doesn't matter if it's the Bible, Book of Mormon, Doctrine and Covenants, or Pearl of Great Price.

They come to us from family and friends who saw us, knew us, and were specifically guided by God to write encouragement, counsel, and love to each of us for our specific time.

Some may say that it's hard to relate to "a bunch of old people who didn't have technology and spoke with a different vocabulary than we do today," but what if those "old people" wrote what they did because they had a special knowledge of *your* circumstances?

Would you read their letters?

Would you search their words again and again?

Would you treasure their letters and keep them safe?

Temple Attendance

President Monson tenderly noted, "As we touch the temple and love the temple, our lives will reflect our faith. As we go to the holy house, as we remember the covenants we make therein, we will be able to bear every trial and overcome each temptation."[6]

Coming home from the MTC allowed me many hours to do what I wanted to do. I received a calling to work in the baptistry at the Draper Utah temple. It was within these sacred walls on Friday mornings that I was able to more fully experience Christ's love for me.

The temple truly is a holy place. It is a place where our soul becomes reenergized, even if we are physically or emotionally exhausted.

I once heard someone say that the Lord holds in special reserve the most sacred of promptings for His children until they come and listen in His home. Though I believe the Lord can speak to us anywhere, the principle of that thought stuck with me. It is within the walls of His home that we truly feel of a *special* Spirit, one that can't be easily replicated anywhere else.

President Hinckley added his testimony on temple work: "Just as our Redeemer gave His life as a vicarious sacrifice for all men, and in so doing became our Savior, even so we, in a small measure, when we engage in proxy work in the temple, become as saviors to those on the other side."[7]

We have a sacred assurance from a prophet of the Lord that when we attend the temple, the people we help to come closer to Christ will inevitably be close to us in return. I like to think of the people whose work I've helped to perform in the temple, if they choose to accept it, are my guardian angels forever. They will help me, because I helped them.

Regardless of any mental, emotional, or physical challenges you may be facing, whether it's struggling with a testimony, feeling you aren't enough due to certain weaknesses or temptations, or dealing with the crutch of perfectionism, you can receive guidance, help, and *peace* as you worship in the House of the Lord.

I'd like to add a special side note for those who may not have a current temple recommend due to individual circumstances. You can rest assured that the Lord sees your investment. Keep a picture of your favorite temple in your bedroom or office. If possible, go to the temple grounds. Go inside the temple and sit in the foyer. You'll be led and guided all the same. The Lord is proud of your desire and your progress.

Service to Others

Mother Teresa taught, "At the end of life we will not be judged by how many diplomas we have received, how much money we have made, how many great things we have done. We will be judged by 'I was hungry, and you gave me something to eat, I was naked and you clothed me. I was homeless, and you took me in.'"[8]

Service to others is one the most ennobling and enabling things we can do on this earth. It doesn't require heavy lifting or operating dangerous machinery (most of the time). It simply requires our hearts and our attitudes. As was discussed in chapter one, missionary service is an act of love for our fellow travelers on this mortal journey, and that service shouldn't end when the badge is removed from our chests or if it was never put there in the first place.

When I was a senior in high school, my friends and I were all in the same seminary class. Our teacher was a prolific author and speaker within the Latter-day Saint community. One day he was teaching the class a lesson about serving those around us who may go unnoticed or unappreciated.

He told a story of how when he was in high school, everyone got together to watch The Lion King one night. He and his friends were all there . . . except one. This particular person had been struggling with family issues for some time and hadn't really been involved in many activities. They were concerned about her and wanted her to feel like she mattered, even though she couldn't be there in person. They decided to go to the nearest grocery store to grab a small bouquet of flowers and a cheerful card to drop off at her home. As a group, they wrote what they liked and missed about this particular person and signed it *The Secret Service.* They dropped it off on her doorstep, rang the doorbell, and ran!

The next day at school, the girl who received the note was visibly moved by it. She told her friends that the night before she was sitting on her couch with her mother who was ill, when suddenly, the doorbell rang. As she answered the door and looked down, she saw some flowers with a card. She thought it was for her mom, but when she opened the card, she saw words of encouragement and love written to her. She was shocked! She broke down and said a prayer of gratitude for whoever dropped off the kind gift.

As she told this story, my seminary teacher and his friends looked at each other with a soft smile. They had done something good, and they knew it. It was especially fulfilling since they did it anonymously.

This story inspired me so much that after school that day I got two of my friends together and we started our own version of The Secret Service. A particular girl we knew was having rough days at school that week, so we went to the grocery store, got some flowers and a card, wrote down some things we admired about her, dropped it off, and booked it down the street in my friend's 2002 Toyota Camry.

Throughout the next few weeks, we tried to be particularly aware and cognizant of those around us at school that might be struggling or discouraged. We kept a list. We got their addresses, and then we served.

I don't know what feels better, knowing that we might have helped someone feel more valued and loved, or knowing that they never found out who it was that left the flowers and cards on their doorsteps. Thank you to my seminary teacher.

Service brings smiles, not only for those who receive it, but also for those who give it. Five years later, I still remember the joy I felt after each time that we anonymously helped someone in need.

When it comes to service, it's the little things.

It doesn't need to be expensive or extravagant. It's the kind thought. It's the word of appreciation. It's the "we're thinking of you" text. Start your own Secret Service. Get your friends together and think about who needs a helping hand or a friendly note, and don't worry about who gets the credit. You'll discover that as you serve without thinking of the recognition you'll receive, your own life, and the lives of those around you, will be more meaningful, happy, and rewarding.

SEEKING PROFESSIONAL HELP

Many have heard the stigma's surrounding people going to see a therapist or counselor for anxiety, depression, or addiction. They're labeled as "people who just need to toughen up" or "people who are just too sensitive for the *real* world," or they're seen as people who have "problems." (Really? Like not all of us have problems?) These labels are false, and they do nothing but discourage people from seeking therapy that could change their lives in a positive way. For those who may spread these falsehoods, I would ask that you please stop. They don't help solve the problem.

You wouldn't tell someone who just broke their leg or tore their ACL that they're wimps for going to the hospital. It's the same thing for emotional health.

As Elder Holland described in his conference address titled, "Like a Broken Vessel":

> [It's] an affliction so severe that it significantly restricts a person's ability to function fully, a crater in the mind so deep that no one can responsibly suggest it would surely go away if those victims would just square their shoulders and think more positively.[9]

When I returned home, my stake patriarch, who happened to be a therapist at the missionary clinic in Salt Lake City, suggested that I set up an appointment to come see him and a psychiatrist as soon as I could. I got into see the therapist quickly, but the psychiatrist would take over a month to get into.

If you're wondering, I didn't want to go to counseling. I had the paradigm I just told you not to have. I didn't want people thinking I was "weak" or "not strong enough to do it on my own." I wanted to do what I had been taught my entire life—get the job done, regardless of how you *feel* about it. However, due to the severity of my condition and the protocol for missionaries who come home early but want to go back into the mission field, I went.

It ended up saving my life.

The first time I went in, the therapist gave me a questionnaire. It involved numerous questions to gauge where I was at in terms of severity with my depressive, manic, and anxious symptoms. After taking it and adding up all my scores (knowing that the lower the score, the lesser the illness), I got a 77/88 . . . not great. My heart was racing as I went back into this older gentleman's office. My first therapy visit had begun.

Sixty minutes later, I walked out feeling as if I could conquer the world. I felt validated, comforted, assured, and helped. The man understood my illness and told me that it was okay to feel as I did. I was going to get help. The road would to be difficult, but I would make it.

I ended up visiting with him every other week for the next year and a half, sharing tears, feelings of inadequacy, feelings of vulnerability, and moments of pure joy.

The next month I was able to visit with the psychiatrist. He is one of my best friends and the man I credit with saving my life. Through over fifty visits, countless discussions, and four different medications, he was by my side teaching me, helping me, and healing me.

Though these men were godsends to me, the road was difficult. When a medication didn't work and my body rejected it, my emotions hit rock bottom. Feelings of suicide occasionally swept over my fractured emotional skeleton. My mental state, mixed with societal pressures and expectations, often brought me to lie on my bedroom floor for hours weeping. As vulnerable as sharing my personal experience is, it's real. Those who experience mental and emotional trauma deal with it constantly.

So, what can you do if someone you know is struggling with mental or emotional illness? Don't belittle, demean, or accuse them of "not being tough enough." Listen to their feelings and their heartache and then validate and support them, perhaps even—and especially—if you haven't experienced those things. Encourage them to see a trusted professional. Worst case scenario: they go for a visit and realize that therapy isn't something they need or enjoy and must find another way to deal with their circumstances. Best case scenario: their life is revolutionized through medication, they find someone to talk to and be vulnerable with, and they go conquer the world. By the time I walked out of my last visit with the doctor a year and half after the start of therapy, my questionnaire score was eleven.

I've known far too many people who could've accepted professional help, but through pride, ignorance, the opinions of others, or lack of knowledge, didn't, and their lives either ended tragically with suicide, or they and their loved ones are still suffering immeasurably.

It doesn't matter who you are or where you're from, therapy is a blessing from a loving Heavenly Father.

And medication is a blessing from a loving Heavenly Father.

You are a blessing from your Heavenly Father to help someone in need.

You are brave. You are loved. You are going to make it.

NOTES

1. Mel Johnson, "Pastor Uses a Glass of Water to Teach Complaining Woman a Lesson." See Godupdates.com, 2017, www.godupdates.com/pastor-glass-of-water-focus-parable/. Accessed June 16, 2020.
2. See goodreads.com/quotes/14500-that-which-we-persist-in-doing-becomes-easier-to-do. Accessed June 16, 2020.
3. W. W. Phelps, "Praise to the Man," *Hymns*, no. 27.
4. *Lincoln Observed: The Civil War Dispatches of Noah Brooks,* edited by Michael Burlingame (Baltimore: Johns Hopkins University Press, 1998), 210.
5. *Teachings of Presidents of the Church: Spencer W. Kimball* (Salt Lake City: The Church of Jesus Christ of Latter-day Saints, 2006), 59–68.
6. Thomas S. Monson, "Blessings of the Temple," *Ensign*, Oct. 2010. See lds.org/study/ensign/2010/10/blessings-of-the-temple?lang=eng. Accessed June 16, 2020.
7. Gordon B. Hinckley, "Closing Remarks," *Ensign*, Nov. 2004. See lds.org/general-conference/2004/10/closing-remarks?lang=eng. Accessed June 16, 2020.
8. See goodreads.com/quotes/759-at-the-end-of-life-we-will-not-be-judged?page=7. Accessed June 16, 2020.
9. *Ensign*, Nov. 2013.

CHAPTER 7

THE FATHER OF ALL LIES

The last thing I want to do is to speak of the devil and give him place in any conversation, but in order to best serve those who read this book, I feel the need to include a chapter on his power and tactics and how to recognize them and defeat him.

First off, missionary work is hard. There are moments when you find yourself at your lowest of lows, not knowing if you can go on. Doors are slammed in your face, you are spit on, reviled, and told you are nothing—all of which can wear on your spirit. Add to that a mental illness, and it borders on almost impossible. The same goes for moments in our everyday lives when we are treated unfairly or feel downtrodden.

Satan loves these moments. He loves when things are hard for us, because that means he has greater capacity to "get us when we're down." I don't know about you, but I've never experienced much temptation when my health is great, the Lord's Spirit is strong, and all my relationships are going perfectly well. In my experience, the slithering snake comes when I've been treated unkindly or when it's been a long day and my soul and body are exhausted.

Satan is a liar. The scriptures denote him as "the adversary," "the devil," "the great deceiver," "the father of all lies," "the father of contention," and so on. (See "Satan" in the King James Version of the Bible in the Bible Dictionary). His main purpose is to make men and women unhappy, unfaithful, unbecoming, and untrue, and he loves to work on missionaries or anyone for that matter who is trying to live their best and help others.

One of Satan's primary weapons is discouragement. Whether we've just sinned, flunked a test, been rejected, or had an argument with a friend, what's one of the first emotions that we feel? Discouragement. Just as President Ezra Taft Benson said, "Satan is increasingly striving to overcome the Saints with despair, discouragement, despondency, and depression."[1]

The first six months that I was home turned out to be the most difficult of my life, and Satan was in my ear the entire time, not just putting bad things into my mind, but also trying to keep good things out. The book *The Screwtape Letters* by C. S. Lewis denotes this scenario almost perfectly. When the senior demon, Screwtape, is teaching his nephew, Wormwood, how to tempt humans better: "It is funny how mortals always picture us as putting things into their minds: in reality our best work is done by keeping things out."[2]

During this time, I learned a valuable lesson: Satan has many ways of tempting, discouraging, and deceiving, but he primarily uses a select few based on the person he's "working" on. The three greatest lies he fed me were

1. You're not worthy
2. You're not good enough
3. Everyone is judging you

Though the three "lies" I experienced may differ from yours, I doubt there isn't one person who hasn't dealt with these before. My purpose in writing this section is to let those who suffer with these lies know that they are not alone and that together we can recognize, combat, and defeat them.

YOU'RE NOT WORTHY

We've all had this feeling before. It doesn't matter if we're a covenant keeper or a deliberate sinner, the lie of "you're not worthy" can linger in our minds. The truth is that there is a succinct difference between "worth" and "worthiness."

No matter what we do, our worth in the sight of God will never change.

We are His children, His precious ones, and His beloved sons and daughters. We may choose to consciously rebel against Christ, the prophet, and the doctrine of The Church of Jesus Christ of Latter-day Saints, but our worth will never change. Christ forever ingrained our worth into our souls when he paid the unfathomable price of atoning for our sins, and nothing we do or don't do will ever change that.

Worthiness, on the other hand, is conditional upon our choices.

We've all heard the scripture, "No unclean thing can dwell in the presence of God" (1 Nephi 10:21). When we sin, fall short, make a mistake, profane (especially during road rage), or give into temptation, we are ultimately choosing to lessen our worthiness. On the other hand, when we repent (turn away from sin and turn back toward God), serve, choose to be kind, "lift the heads that hang down and strengthen the feeble knees" (Doctrine and Covenants 81:5), our worthiness increases through the blood of Jesus Christ.

To Satan, all of God's children are seen as the same thing: bait. He doesn't care if we are a bishop or a drug addict, he will attack us constantly with feelings of worthlessness. Why? Because he wants to keep us away from thinking about who we *really* are: sons and daughters of Heavenly Parents with the potential to become God's and Goddesses and create worlds without end.

As obvious as this sounds, the more we think we aren't worthy, the less we think about Christ.

So, as soon as we start questioning ourselves, let us first be reminded that our worth is eternal and will never change. If we are worrying about our worthiness, we need to diagnose where those feelings are coming from. If we feel discouraged, confused, or scared about our feelings of worthiness, then they are most likely coming from Satan. On the other hand, if we are feeling peace, regardless of how scared we are, we can know it's God working through us, for although Satan can deceive in many emotions, he can never give us a feeling of peace.

YOU'RE NOT GOOD ENOUGH

Raise your hand if you've ever felt this way. Seems like in our culture of perfectionism, this is one of the most talked about and frequently felt deceptions there is. Although I numbered this second, it has always had the strongest impact on me. Perhaps my own perfectionism prompts it, but regardless, anyone who has ever tried to live the commandments has felt they were not *good* enough.

How ironic it is that the devil, who never wants us to attain perfection, often tempts us with thoughts of becoming perfect.

In a world where you can filter anything or alter any physical imperfection with surgery or cosmetics, it's hard *not* to feel the pressure to be perfect. I don't blame those of us who constantly struggle with this thought that they are never good enough, because we are implicitly taught that our whole lives.

Here are some real-life examples (not all specific to Latter-day Saint culture) of how we've been taught to hide our imperfections to make it come across like we are perfect:

- A young woman sees on social media that she isn't naturally pretty enough, so she decides to take laxatives and get fake body enhancements to get that "perfect figure" and live up to unrealistic expectations.

- Parents and leaders teaching younger children that sinning is bad and should be avoided at all costs without emphasizing what to do *when* they sin (because we all do), creating a false paradigm in the children's mind that confession and repentance are scary, judgmental, and should only be a last resort.

- Men being taught not to show emotion since it comes across as a sign of weakness, so they hide and bottle up their true feelings, creating an inevitable explosion that might end up hurting themselves and those they love.

- Parents of similar faiths keeping their kids from interacting with those of opposite faiths to not "risk" the possibility of the kids being indoctrinated in a *false* religion. (I've seen this firsthand in my own life.)

- Parents telling their children that regardless of anything they do in life, serving a mission for The Church of Jesus Christ of Latter-day Saints is one of the only things that matter. Because of this, even if a child is terrified, lacks a testimony, or is clinically depressed, that child will suppress their true feelings, not tell anyone since it makes them appear weak or "unspiritual," and submit their mission papers anyway in order to fulfill the unrealistic expectations put upon them.

Now, these may come across as extreme, and I'm sure all these examples have underlying intentions of love and care, but you get the gist. Of course, not all women on social media feel that way. Of course, parents and leaders want to keep children away from sin and experiences that could harm them. Of course, some men have the courage to be vulnerable. Of course, parents aren't trying to limit their children's opportunities to make friends. Of course, a parent wants the best for their child and is just trying to encourage and promote the life-changing experiences a mission can bring.

We need to be careful how we declare our intent, even if we *think* it's the best for that person. When we try to push our will on another person or don't try to understand how the other person feels, we can be setting them up for a lifelong battle of feeling, "I'll just never be good enough unless I can do every single thing I've been taught by my parents and leaders." Though this may come as a shock to many, I'll share what my therapist told me when I expressed my distress with never being able to live up to unrealistic expectations set upon me by those who cared for me the most: "Drew, your parents are not God. Your leaders are not God. They are wonderful and trusting and want the best for you, but they are not God. God is God. His voice is the one that matters most."

So, what can we do when we don't feel good enough? Ask God how He feels about you, how you are doing, and what, if anything, you need to stop doing or start doing to make sure you're accomplishing *your* mission. Then listen. Act and be confident in yourself.

Though everyone wanted what was best for me when I returned home early, I never felt good enough. I never felt I was doing what they wanted or expected of me. Have you ever felt this way?

No one ever told me that I had fulfilled my missionary service after two months. Where did I receive that confirmation? From the only One who could fill me with indescribable peace and the courage to resolve the conflicts that were whirling inside of me: God.

If you are not God—and you're not—then understand that maybe the way you did things growing up isn't the path for the person you are trying to help.

Just because you are a doctor doesn't mean the person coming to you for career advice should be a doctor. Even though your oldest daughter had a life-changing experience on her mission doesn't mean your youngest daughter should serve a mission. Your closest friend might have a cute boyfriend, but that doesn't mean you need to date someone to feel good about yourself. Even though you studied tirelessly to become valedictorian and get into a prestigious college doesn't mean that your best friend or younger sibling needs to do the exact same thing. And just because you know someone who started their family when they were twenty-two doesn't mean you have to. The list goes on and on with examples of potential opportunities to force our agenda on someone else . . . but it's not what we should do.

What we can do is to respectfully—and lovingly—empathize and understand what the person we are trying to help is going through. Then we can encourage them to do what is *right for them and their circumstances.* One of the most wonderful things about being a member of The Church of Jesus Christ of Latter-day Saints is that we have an entire community, seventeen million strong, that want the best for each other. We all want to help each other succeed. We all want those around us to reach their highest potential. That's admirable! But we need to realize that in the process of helping someone reach his or her potential, we shouldn't put our agenda or time line on them.

Everyone has their own mission, and the greatest gift we can give someone is to help them discover that mission for themselves.

EVERYONE IS JUDGING YOU

What's one of the most common things we do as humans when we mess up? Though I wish everyone would respond, "Take responsibility and own up to our actions," that's usually not how it goes. We usually try to hide it, and by hiding it, we consequently isolate ourselves from others. Satan loves this. He loves when we are alone. He loves when we feel that we can't talk to people about things or confide in our loved ones. He loves when we think everyone is out to get us or that everyone gossips about us constantly. This is the last of the three deceptions he tried to nail me with when I returned home.

From the first Sunday when I entered the meeting house doors and saw everyone's eyes turn to me with puzzled looks on their faces, I thought one thing: "They're all judging me." This belief system, which wasn't true, made it difficult for me to talk to, trust, and get along with others because I thought they were thinking of me as a failure, a screw-up, and a sinner. I isolated myself. I lost my love for others and for life. It impacted me, not only emotionally but also physically.

Now, I know that some people *were* judging me. It's easy to tell when someone you know well doesn't approve of what you're doing or your lifestyle. But not *everyone* was judging me. I actually had quite a few champions who were pulling for me and encouraging me to heal, to get control of my life and do what was best for me, not just what everyone else thought I should do. However, the "mists of darkness" (1 Nephi 12:17) were hard to see through at the time.

And that's the point of this third deception that Satan used on me and uses on each of us. Some people are outright jerks or latter-day Pharisees, but most people aren't as judgmental as we sometimes think they are. As hard as this is to believe, most people are too busy with families, personal issues, and overall life to devote extra energy to focusing on another person's life.

To quote Stephen R. Covey, author of the book *7 Habits of Highly Effective People,* "We see the world not as it is, but as we are."[3]

If we believe that no one is good, that we are constantly under scrutiny, that people are talking about us behind our backs, then that is how we will live. We won't trust people. We won't create fulfilling relationships. We won't want to help others. This is what happened to me for at least six months after I came home.

So, what turned things around? I learned something about judgment, particularly righteous judgment. I learned that it didn't matter what people thought about me. In the words of President Joseph Smith, "I knew it, and I knew that God knew it, and I could not deny it."[4]

What can we as neighbors, families, and friends do to judge righteously but at the same time not become a gossiper or delve into things (other people's lives) that aren't our business?

Elder Holland said,

> In this regard—this call for compassion and loyalty to the commandments—there is sometimes a chance for a misunderstanding, especially among young people who may think we are not supposed to judge anything, that we are never to make a value assessment of any kind. We have to help each other with that because the Savior makes it clear that in some situations we *have* to judge, we are under obligation to judge—as when He said, "Give not that which is holy unto the dogs, neither cast ye your pearls before swine" (Matthew 7:6). That sounds like a judgment to me.[5]

In this process of evaluation, we are not called on to *condemn* others, but we are called upon to make decisions every day that reflect judgment—we hope good judgment. Elder Dallin H. Oaks once referred to these kinds of decisions as "intermediate judgments," which we often have to make for our own safety or for the safety of others as opposed to what he called "final judgments," which can only be made by God, who knows all the facts.[6]

Remember that the Savior said these are to be "righteous judgments," *not* self-righteous judgments, which is a very different thing.

When we see someone choose not to take the sacrament or notice that someone hasn't come to Church in awhile, or when we learn that our best friend is taking medication or that someone has come home early from missionary service, if we choose to judge them, we are doing it self-righteously, not righteously. We are judging them through our paradigm of how we think things are *supposed* to be. Not only is it none of our business, but there is also a lot of behind-the-scenes information that we know nothing about. Let the Lord handle those judgments. Let's focus our attention on loving and building ourselves and strive to lift others along the way.

_____

NOTES

1. Ezra Taft Benson, "Do Not Despair," *Ensign*, Oct. 1986, 4.
2. C. S. Lewis, *The Screwtape Letters* (San Francisco: HarperOne, 2015).
3. Stephen R. Covey, *The 7 Habits of Highly Effective People* (New York: Free Press, 1989).
4. Joseph Smith—History 1:25.
5. Jeffrey R. Holland, "Conviction with Compassion," *New Era*, July 2013. Adapted from a CES devotional given on September 9, 2012, titled "Israel, Israel, God Is Calling."
6. See Dallin H. Oaks, "'Judge Not' and Judging," *Ensign*, Aug. 1999, 6–13.

CHAPTER 8

I AM THE LIGHT OF THE WORLD

If it wasn't for Jesus Christ, our purpose in mortality would be utterly pointless, and we would forever be subject to the devil (2 Nephi 9:9). It is because of Christ that those who decide to serve missions can go. His name is on our name tags, and, more important, on our hearts. We owe everything to Him.

As mentioned in the previous chapter, discovering our mission in life can be challenging. We may be deceived and succumb to temptation at times. We won't be proud of it, and we will most likely look back and wonder what in the world we were thinking, but we can be assured that with Christ "all things are possible" (Matthew 19:26). We can repent, learn, grow, and continue to move forward on the gospel path until we return to Him again.

Just as Satan feeds us three lies to confuse us in challenging moments, Jesus Christ offers us three truths to give us peace during those challenging moments. They are

1. Be kind to yourself
2. Direction is more important than speed
3. Focus on what matters most

Though Satan is good at yelling and attracting attention through anger (Moses 1:19–22), Christ can pierce us to the very core with peace (3 Nephi 11:3), causing us to feel, see, and hear exactly what is needed.

BE KIND TO YOURSELF

In an interview produced by The Church of Jesus Christ of Latter-day Saints, President Russell M. Nelson admonished, "Don't demand of yourself things that are unreasonable, but demand of yourself improvement . . . perfection comes not in this life, but the next life."[1]

Elder Devin Cornish added to that by saying, "Please sincerely ask Him what He thinks of you. He will love and correct but never discourage us; that is Satan's trick."[2]

President Uchtdorf also testified, "The heavens will not be filled with those who never made mistakes but with those who recognized that they were off course and who corrected their ways to get back in the light of gospel truth."[3]

Perhaps it's the perfectionism within all of us, but it seems as if there's always a voice inside of us saying, "You won't get anywhere in life unless you beat yourself up and tell yourself you're never going to be good enough."

It seems ironic, doesn't it? How could we ever get somewhere in life by beating ourselves up? I think the answer is simple—we can't. If we did, we wouldn't last long since our self-esteem would be so low.

Negative self-talk is another one of Satan's strongest tools. I've known many friends who, after scoring 89 percent (B plus) on a test in school, think, "Oh, I'm such an idiot. If I had only gotten one more question right, I would've had an A minus! I'm never going to be successful." (As if getting one more question right would alter their entire life trajectory.) Sound harsh? Well, speaking from personal experience, it's what a lot of us experience in different ways.

I'm not discounting those who have high expectations for themselves or their loved ones, but there comes a time when you need to step back and tell yourself, "You know what, I'm not where I want to be *yet*, but I'm a lot farther along than I was a year ago." That's called having a growth mindset.

Carol Dweck, author of the book *Mindset: The New Psychology of Success* and professor at Stanford University, has helped children struggling with negative self-esteem, self-talk, and anxiety bounce out of discouragement and recognize that they are doing better than they think they. She believes there is a difference between a fixed mindset and a growth mindset.[4]

People with a fixed mindset think their characteristics are carved in stone and can never be changed. They firmly believe that intelligence, creativity, and personality are things we are born with that can't be developed or improved. They want results right away and don't care as much about the process as they do the outcome.

People with a growth mindset, however, believe we can cultivate these characteristics through effort, persistence, and determination, and who we become in pursuit of our goals is more important than the outcome of reaching them.

Carol is currently working with school districts across the country. Instead of giving children failing grades, she suggests giving them "not yet" grades. She believes that when we tell children they have failed an assignment, they think of themselves as a failure, which can lead to adulthood negativity and anxiety. This creates a fixed mindset. On the other hand, when we tell children that they haven't learned it "yet," we are building a foundation upon which they can progress and learn from their mistakes until they can move on to the next challenge, which creates a growth mindset.

How can you help cultivate a growth mindset in your friends, family members, or church associates? How can you bring the power of "not yet" into the lives of those around you?

When I returned home from the MTC, I had a fixed mindset, and that led me to believe I was never going to succeed in life because of this one experience. Then one day I found a letter on my pillow from my brother that reminded me of the power of self-love.

In essence it said, "We all go through hard things in life that can test us, and even though I don't know what you had to go through at the MTC, I know that this will make you better as a person, and you will get back on top. Sometimes I get so mad at myself for things I've done, or for messing up, but I'm telling you, be kind to yourself. You will do great things with your life."

Last, in speaking about being kind to oneself, President Gordon B. Hinckley offered these words of comfort: "Please don't nag yourselves with thoughts of failure. Do not set goals far beyond your capacity to achieve. Simply do what you can do, in the best way you know how, and the Lord will accept your effort."[5]

DIRECTION IS MORE IMPORTANT THAN SPEED

Elder Larry W. Lawrence said, "To Him, our direction is more important than our speed."[6]

It is true that if you're pointed in the wrong direction, it doesn't matter how fast you're traveling. Inversely, if you're locked on to your desired destination, all progress is positive, no matter how slow you're going. You'll reach your goal eventually. These are wise words indeed!

King Benjamin described this principle of direction over speed when he said, "And see that all these things are done in wisdom and order; for it is not requisite that a man should run faster than he has strength. And again, it is expedient that he should be diligent, that thereby he might win the prize; therefore, all things must be done in order" (Mosiah 4:27).

I don't know where the notion came from that implies that if you're not first, you're last, and that if you're not exhausted, you're not doing it right. I don't know of any scripture or prophetic teaching that tells us to run to the finish line, go as fast as we can, and make sure we are spiritually exhausted with all the service we are doing; otherwise, we won't make it to the celestial kingdom.

The Lord explicitly tells us that it is not required (requisite) for us to run faster than we are able, but it is very important (expedient) that we are going in the right direction and are diligent, otherwise we may miss the mark.

As children of Heavenly Parents, we often tell ourselves that because this life is the time to "prepare," there is no preparation on the other side of the veil. That's not true. Satan wants us to think that it's all or nothing, that if we don't make it to the end of this life, panting, crying, and discouraged from how spiritually inadequate we are, we'll be excluded from heaven. Lies, lies, lies!

Elder Bruce R. McConkie countered this satanic lie of "speed is what matters most" when he said,

> We don't need to get a complex or get a feeling that you have to be perfect to be saved. You don't. There's only been one perfect person, and that's the Lord Jesus, but in order to be saved in the Kingdom of God and in order to pass the test of mortality, what you have to do is get on the straight and narrow path . . . and then, being on that path, pass out of this life in full fellowship. I'm not saying that you don't have to keep the command-ments. I'm saying you don't have to be perfect to be saved. If you did, no one would be saved. The way it operates is this: you get on the path that's named the "straight and narrow." You do it by entering the gate of repentance and baptism. The straight and narrow path leads from the gate of repentance and baptism, a very great distance, to a reward that's called eternal life. If you're on that path and pressing forward, and you die, you'll never get off the path. There is no such thing as falling off the straight and narrow path in the life to come, and the reason is that this life is the time that is given to men to prepare for eternity. Now is the time and the day of your salvation, so if you're working zealously in this life—though you haven't fully overcome the world and you haven't done all you hoped you might do—you're still going to be saved. You don't

have to do what Jacob said, "Go beyond the mark." You don't have to live a life that's truer than true. You don't have to have an excessive zeal that becomes fanatical and becomes unbalancing. What you have to do is stay in the mainstream of the Church and live as upright and decent people live in the Church—keeping the commandments, paying your tithing, serving in the organizations of the Church, loving the Lord, staying on the straight and narrow path.[7]

Because of my experience, I thought all missionaries who went into the field were getting a "two year" head start on me spiritually. They would somehow be "better" at life because they had this experience and I didn't. They were growing "faster" than I was and would be worthier and more capable. These thoughts weighed on me for months, because I didn't realize that God cared more about my direction than my speed.

He cared more about which way I faced than how fast I was going. If someone joins the Church at age fifty instead of twenty, are they thirty years "behind"? Of course not. They are on their own path, and there should be no comparing when it comes to their walk with Christ.

Whether we think we are falling behind spiritually due to mental, emotional, or physical debilitations; someone else's choices; or our own mistakes, the words of Elder McConkie apply to everyone's circumstances *now*.

The gospel is simple, even when we may not see it as such.

When it comes to this life, we *won't* be perfect, and that is perfectly fine.

We can make sure that regardless of our speed or the speed of those around us, our direction can be pointed toward Him who is the "giver of every good gift" (James 1:17).

FOCUS ON THE THINGS THAT MATTER MOST

Elder Dieter F. Uchtdorf once shared a message that has had an eternal impact on me. In his message, he told a story about trees and airplane turbulence. He said, "When weather, soil, and environmental conditions for trees are ideal, they grow at a normal rate. However, when those conditions are not ideal, trees slow down their growth to take care of the basic necessities."

He continued to talk about airplanes, and how many of us have experienced this shaky and uncomfortable sensation flying at thirty thousand feet. In combatting this turbulence, pilots should do two things: First, an inexperienced pilot may think it's wise to speed up and try to get through the turbulence faster, but this is unwise and potentially dangerous. An experienced pilot will slow the plane and focus on getting through the turbulence safely and optimally. "Therefore," Elder Uchtdorf said, "it is good advice to slow down a little, steady the course, and focus on the essentials when experiencing adverse conditions."[8]

Just as direction is more important than speed, it is more important to focus on the things that matter most when we are going through difficult, stressful, or challenging seasons in our lives. Satan would have us scrambling every minute of every day doing menial tasks that yield little to no results, while Jesus would have us do the simple things and devote our time and attention to those that have the greatest impact on our lives. This includes our relationships with family and friends, God, and oneself.

Elder Uchtdorf counseled,

Isn't it true that we often get so busy? And, sad to say, we even wear our busyness as a badge of honor, as though being busy, by itself, was an accomplishment or sign of a superior life.

Is it?

I think of our Lord and Exemplar, Jesus Christ, and His short life among the people of Galilee and Jerusalem. I have tried to imagine Him bustling between meetings or multitasking to get a list of urgent things accomplished.

I can't see it.

Instead, I see the compassionate and caring Son of God purposefully living each day. When He interacted with those around Him, they felt important and loved. He gave them the precious gift of His time.[9]

One may try to counter this by saying, "You don't understand. I *have* to be busy. I have a full-time job, I'm in school, I have family that needs me, and I have civic responsibilities. On top of that, I need to take care of myself. There just isn't enough time in the day to focus on the things that matter most."

But that's just it. We can learn to focus on the things that matter most by using small, bite-size chunks throughout the day to build our relationships with others, God, and ourselves. By focusing on the things that matter most, the Lord isn't telling us to neglect our jobs, our community, or our responsibilities. He is simply telling us to put our most precious efforts into the things that last the longest.

Julie B. Beck once said something that impacted the way I see spiritual things: "Spend time in the scriptures every day."[10]

Now, she didn't say *how much* time to spend in them; she just said to spend time in them. We are to use the Spirit and our own judgment according to our personal circumstances to determine how long we engage in spiritual things. What matters most, however, is that we put in the effort to do it.

Renowned time-management specialist, parenting expert, and numerous *New York Times* best-selling author Julie Morgenstern explained in her seminal book *Time to Parent*: "What humans need—little humans and big humans—are short bursts of undivided attention delivered consistently."

She explains that we often think of building relationships as this long, tedious, hour-upon-hour job, when in reality it can be done quite simply by giving our undivided attention to someone for five to ten minutes at a time, five times a day. This includes when we wake up, when we leave for work or school, when we come home, after dinner, and right at bedtime.[11]

When the Lord invites us to focus on the things that matter most, He is asking us to look at what we spend our time on, if it is consistent with what we truly believe, and then to decide what we need to keep doing or stop doing.

Jim Rohn, a great business philosopher, said, "What's easy to do is easy not to do."[12]

Profound. Simple. Easy to understand.

It's easy to pray. It's easy to take five minutes with your spouse or best friend and give them your undivided attention. It's easy to take a walk or go for a bike ride to preserve your health. It's easy to read a good book for ten minutes a day. It's easy to choose the apple over the oreo. . . . But, it's also easy *not* to do those things. It's easy to forget. It's easy to become distracted and complacent.

So, what can we do to focus on the things that matter most? May I offer this simple three-step formula:

1. Look at your life and see how you spend your time.
2. Decide if what you do every day is consistent with what you truly believe matters most.
3. Ask God to help you start doing the right things and stop doing the wrong things.

NOTES

1. Russell M. Nelson, "Men's Hearts Shall Fail Them." See churchofjesuschrist. org/inspiration/latter-day-saints-channel/. Accessed June 16, 2020.
2. J. Devin Cornish, "Am I Good Enough? Will I Make It?" *Ensign,* Nov. 2016, 33.
3. Dieter F. Uchtdorf, "A Matter of a Few Degrees," *Ensign*, May 2008.
4. Carol Dweck, *Mindset: The New Psychology of Success*, updated edition (New York: Ballantine Books, 2007).
5. Gordon B. Hinckley, "Rise to the Stature of the Divine within You," *Ensign*, Nov. 1989.
6. Larry R. Lawrence, "What Lack I Yet?," *Ensign*, Nov. 2015.
7. Bruce R. McConkie, "The Probationary Test of Mortality," Salt Lake Institute of Religion devotional, Jan. 10, 1982, 12–13.
8. Dieter F. Uchtdorf, "Of Things That Matter Most," *Ensign*, Nov. 2010.
9. Ibid., "Of Regrets and Resolutions," *Ensign*, Nov. 2012.
10. Julie B. Beck, "My Soul Delighteth in the Scriptures," *Ensign*, May 2004.
11. Julie Morgenstern, *Time to Parent: Organizing Your Life to Bring Out the Best in Your Child and You* (New York: Henry Holt and Company, 2018).
12. Jim Rohn, *The Day That Turns Your Life Around*, audio (Wheeling, IL: Nightingale-Conant, 2003).

CHAPTER 9

ANATOMY OF A MISSION CALL

For anyone who has taken a human anatomy class in school, they know it can be difficult. It isn't a simple "look around and you're done" type class. It is strenuous and meticulous. It involves digging deep into the human physique and learning about muscles, tendons, and vessels, not just to look at the outer bones and tissues. This chapter aims to do the same. We will look at the anatomy of a mission call, not at surface level, but deeply. We will discuss phrases and words that, if understood, may change the way you and your loved ones view a mission call. We'll talk about what the Lord issues to each of us when we are called to the work and how we can better fulfill our earthly mission as well.

Opening a mission call is one of the most adrenaline-filled experiences a member of The Church of Jesus Christ of Latter-day Saints can have. Most of the time, friends and family gather around, the future missionary stands in front them, and with pin-drop silence, he or she tears open the envelope (or now, I guess, they open it as an email).

As they read the message, everyone hopes the call to serve is issued where they guessed it would be on a big map of the world. In anticipation, the man or woman reads the life-changing words, "You are assigned to labor in the . . ."

Loud shouts echo through the house. Parents cry, and everyone hugs.

What I didn't realize at the time is that receiving a mission call is more than finding out *where* you are going to serve, though it is exciting. It is more about discovering *how* you are going to serve and *why* you are serving. We uncover where we are going to serve in the last paragraph of the mission call, but we uncover *how* and *why* we are to serve in the beginning paragraphs, or, as I like to call it, the *fine print* of a mission call.

With that thought, there are three key phrases that, if read and pondered, would make the experience of receiving a mission call far more sacred and worthwhile, which will give us guidance and a better perspective on how to fulfill our *earthly* mission. These are

1. "Hereby called to serve"
2. "You are assigned to labor"
3. "It is anticipated"

I will be referring to Elder David A. Bednar's talk from the April 2016 general conference titled "Called to the Work" as I discuss the anatomy of a mission call.

"HEREBY CALLED TO SERVE"

"Dear Elder/Sister (blank), you are hereby called to serve as a missionary for The Church of Jesus Christ of Latter-day Saints. You are assigned to labor in the _____ Mission."

My grandpa always used to tell me, "It doesn't matter where you serve, but how you serve." Though on the surface this saying made sense to me, I never understood how important it was for me to understand. Growing up, when I would hear people talk about missionary work, the conversation often went something like this, "So where did you serve your mission? Oh, Russia! Wow, that must've been hard. How many baptisms did you get?"

The emphasis was always first placed on *where* the missionary had a chance to serve, instead of *how* they served. You never realize how big this is culturally until you come home early from missionary service, never having reached the "field," and have to answer people when they ask, "So where did you serve your mission?" As one could guess, this was extremely difficult for me to handle. Because I returned home early, I never got to the "field." I never got to Estonia, so I had no idea how to tell people *where* I served. This wore on me emotionally. I was always concerned with the fact that because I didn't get to go to my "mission call assignment," I must've failed—that is, until I heard Elder Bednar's talk. From his talk, I learned that first, I'm not called to a place. I'm called to serve. And second, the Lord has the ability to "reassign" us for His purposes.

Elder Bednar said, "In the culture of the Church, we often talk of being called to serve in a country such as Argentina, Poland, Korea, or the United States. But a missionary is not called to a place; rather, he or she is called to serve. As the Lord declared through the Prophet Joseph Smith in 1829, 'If ye have desires to serve God ye are called to the work.'"[1]

He went on to recount a story of a man called to serve somewhere but was reassigned due to various reasons and how that affected him:

> When a missionary is reassigned to a different field of labor, the process is precisely the same as for the initial assignment. Members of the Quorum of the Twelve seek inspiration and guidance in making all such reassignments.

> I recently spoke with a faithful man who shared with me the deepest feelings of his heart. In a meeting, I had just explained the difference between being called to the work and assigned to labor. This good brother shook my hand and with tears in his eyes said to me, "The things you helped me learn today have lifted a burden from my shoulders that I have carried for more than 30 years. As a young missionary, I was initially assigned to a field of labor in South America. But I was unable to obtain a visa, so my assignment was changed to the United States. All these years I have wondered why I was unable to serve in the place to which I had been called. Now I know I was called to the work and not to a place. I cannot tell you how much this understanding has helped me."

> My heart ached for this good man . . . I am addressing this subject today because not a single member of this Church should carry an unnecessary burden of misunderstanding, uncertainty, anguish, or guilt about an assignment to labor.[2]

It wasn't until I heard these words that I finally realized that I didn't "come home early from my mission," but rather, I was *reassigned*. Yes, I never made it to Estonia as a full-time missionary, but that's okay. I was "called to the work" in a different place, for a different purpose, and for a different time period.

You are similarly called to your own work where you are now.

In addition to that, I learned that being reassigned doesn't only apply geographically. The Lord can reassign us emotionally, mentally, or physically. You may be highly successful at your job, but then you are fired due to circumstances beyond your control, and you're bitter and angry. Hold on, the Lord is working on your reassignment. You may be a mother who has prayed so long to have a baby and then has a miscarriage, and you just don't understand why. Trust on, the Lord is working on reassigning you too. You may have had a happy childhood, confident in your abilities and relationships, but due to a traumatizing event, you find yourself battling with anxiety or depression. Fear not, the Lord is the master healer and is working on reassigning you. You may have an extremely dedicated work ethic and done well in your studies, but due to events outside of your control, you've been passed over for a scholarship or not been admitted to a school of your choice. Don't worry, the Lord is working to reassign you and your needs right now.

For those of you who may be experiencing feelings of shame, guilt, or sadness due to your own experiences with being "reassigned," may I assure you that the Lord does nothing save it be for the benefit of our souls (2 Nephi 26:24). He is the master healer. He is your creator. It doesn't matter where you serve but how you serve.

"YOU ARE ASSIGNED TO LABOR"

As missionaries, we are assigned to labor. I've often wondered why the Lord used the word "labor" in the mission call. Perhaps it's inconsequential, but then again, the Lord doesn't waste words. Just as each word chosen in an apostle's talk for general conference is meticulous, I would assume the Lord's words are chosen with perfect precision. Why didn't He say, "You are assigned to work," or, "You are assigned to preach"?

Labor is defined, "To exert one's powers of body or mind especially with painful or strenuous effort."[3]

Work is defined as an "activity in which one exerts strength or faculties to do or perform something."[4]

What's the difference between these two words? They both require strength, but "to labor" often comes with "painful or strenuous effort." The Lord isn't just calling us to "work." He's calling us to "labor." He's not just asking for a portion of our hearts and minds, but for everything. He is letting us know, up front, it will be strenuous and painful at times. He is letting us know that a mission will stretch us. It will involve "growing pains." It will bring us to our knees so He can lift us up.

One often hears the phrase, "A mission wasn't the best years of my life, but it was the best years *for* my life." A possible explanation for this statement would most likely be because of the growth experienced.

Growth is good; but growth is hard.

Growth requires discomfort and pain at times. I don't know many people who enjoy being stretched and taken outside of their comfort zone. I certainly don't. One of the main purposes for this earthly experience is to give us opportunities to grow.

But there's only one problem with growth: it's not guaranteed. Take a tree for example. If you put an oak tree seed in the ground, give it enough water, sunlight, and nutrients, what happens? It grows. Not only that, but it also grows through every possible adversity this earth could place in its path. Thunderstorms? No problem. Winds? No problem. Because a tree hasn't been given the dignity of choice, it just grows and grows and grows until it reaches its fullest potential. Humans, on the other hand, have the gift of personal agency. They can choose. They can decide what they do during life's "thunderstorms" and "winds." They can decide if they will persevere and grow, or crumble and give up. What does this mean? It means that humans are the only of God's creations that run the risk of not reaching their fullest potential. All other creatures are ultimately subject to DNA and the genetic code.

When we are "assigned to labor," we are being commissioned by the Savior of the World to grow through the "painful or strenuous effort." We are being commissioned to give Him our hearts, muscles, determination, and love. We are commissioned to simply do our best. That's all. What do we get in return? "Behold, he that thrusteth in his sickle with his might, the same layeth up in store that he perisheth not, but bringeth salvation to his soul" (D&C 4:4). Not only salvation in the next life, but also as much as God can give us will be ours in this life.

The choice is ours. This life is our mission. Will we go through it, or will we *grow* through it?

"IT IS ANTICIPATED"

As much as we are taught to believe in the culture of The Church of Jesus Christ of Latter-day Saints that a mission is a saving ordinance, it's not. It doesn't have the eternal significance that a temple sealing or receiving an endowment does. That does not mean, however, that it is not important. If we so desire and are guided by the Holy Ghost to serve a mission, we absolutely should; otherwise we run the risk of having major regrets for the remainder of our lives. God's ways are higher than our ways, and His plans are much better than our plans, even if we don't think so.

So, He gave us a key phrase in the mission call that is vital not only for those who serve missions for The Church of Jesus Christ of Latter-day Saints, but also for those whose lives are a mission (which applies to everyone on this planet).

"It is anticipated."

Anticipate is defined as "regard as probable; expect or predict."[5]

Of course, as a missionary, you hope and desire that you will serve in the land you were originally called to and for the expected time period, but it's not guaranteed or promised.

Remember, His ways are not our ways . . . and He has a better plan for us. I wish the Latter-day Saint culture understood this. We hope, we expect, and we pray that an individual will serve the "full" time in the field, but what if that isn't God's will? Do we care more about our timetable or His? The same applies to any calling within the Church. If someone is part of the bishopric for only two years, or a member of the relief society presidency only serves for two months then is released, do we raise an eyebrow or do we support them?

Just as we all expect and hope that those we love will live until their eighties or nineties, sometimes their lives end in their forties or fifties. Do we judge people because of that or think they didn't do enough? No. We trust that God had another work for them to do, and we do our best to honor what they did accomplish. It should be no different when it comes to service within the Church.

Notice that the Lord didn't say "it is required" that we serve for a period of time. I believe it's because He knew there would be exceptions of all types and circumstances, planned and unplanned. Does this require us to look at people differently or undermine their worth because they didn't do something we "expected" them to do? I absolutely hope not.

In full transparency, this is something I struggled with. Before I learned this lesson for myself, I tried to push my expectations on others and judged them if they didn't follow through on them. I will share one of those vulnerable experiences, hoping you will learn from it and perhaps avoid my mistake.

Someone very dear to me received a mission call and decided not to go on their mission. It was "anticipated" that they would serve a twenty-four-month mission, but they didn't. Did I look at them differently at the time? Yes. Did I think, *If only I could encourage them enough to go on a mission, I know everything in their life would work out*? Yes. Did I choose to love them for who they were, look for the good in what they did, and encourage them to be the best they could be? Not as much as I should have, and that made a somewhat small impact on our relationship. We grew apart for a few years, and it was my fault. Shame on me. Shame on my limited view of what God has asked us to do, regardless of the choices those around us make . . .

especially when it comes to something that can be so personal and misunderstood. Shame on me for being blind to the fact that God didn't need me to judge but to love and be kind and try to do my personal best instead of focusing so much on someone else's life.

I thank Him for being patient with me. Once I fully grasped this lesson (after having to experience it myself), I never looked at this person in a negative way again. I now see them as my soul mate, an individual with a heart of gold. They would rush to my aid at any time of the day or night, and I would do the same for them. We've laughed together, and we've cried together. They are my spirit sibling, and regardless of what they do or don't do, I will love them and be there for them always.

We expect to have the perfect mission without any problems whatsoever, but that isn't reality.

God is perfect, yes, but missions are not. Sometimes we are "reassigned" as discussed earlier, and sometimes what we "anticipated" just isn't the right thing for our loved ones or us. That doesn't mean we shouldn't be ecstatic to serve, fully hoping that we can give our all in the land of our original assignment. I believe what it does mean is this: The Lord is in control. He knows exactly what we need, and we can rely 100 percent on what He chooses to do with us if our hearts are malleable and our desires are righteous.

As Elder Jeffrey R. Holland testified, "Nothing in this universe is more important to Him than your hopes and dreams."[6]

Now that we've gone over the anatomy of a mission call, the question may be asked, "So now that we know we can be 'reassigned' and it's only 'anticipated' that we will serve in the land of our original mission call, what should we focus on? Should I be excited for the future?" The answer is an unequivocal yes!

Remember, no matter how exciting it is to know *where* and for *how long* you will serve, what matters most is *how* you will serve and *why* you're serving in the first place. We are all emissaries of Christ regardless of whether we have a name tag on our chests.

As Elder Bednar counseled,

Each of you is a missionary now. All around you, every day, are friends and neighbors "who are only kept from the truth because they know not where to find it." As you are directed by the Spirit, you can share a thought, an invitation, a text or tweet that will introduce your friends to the truths of the restored gospel. You need not and should not wait for your official call to become anxiously engaged in missionary work.

In conclusion, let us remember that as missionaries and as individuals, in this life we are not called to places, we are called to serve, and if we can't fulfill the service we've been called to for one reason or another, we haven't failed or fallen short. We've simply been reassigned according to the Lord's plan for us.

Regardless of where we go or for how long we serve (or live), focusing on doing the best we can and letting the Lord multiply our efforts will bring the greatest peace.

Notes

1. David A. Bednar, "Called to the Work," *Ensign*, May 2016.
2. Ibid.
3. Merriam-Webster's Dictionary. See merriam-webster.com/dictionary/labor. Accessed June 16, 2020.
4. Ibid., merriam-webster.com/dictionary/work. Accessed June 16, 2020.
5. Ibid., merriam-webster.com/dictionary/anticipate. Accessed June 16, 2020.
6. Jeffrey R. Holland, "To Young Women," *Ensign*, Nov. 2005.
7. Bednar, "Called to the Work."

CHAPTER 10

LETTING GO OF PERFECTIONISM

Whether you are a missionary who has been reassigned for one reason or another, a convert to the Church, a lifelong disciple, or somewhere in between, we've all had run-ins with the "myth of perfectionism." Though discussed briefly throughout previous chapters of this book, this chapter is devoted strictly to perfectionism, what it is, and how we can overcome it.

First, I believe there is a strong difference between someone who struggles with perfectionism and someone who has an innate desire to be his or her best self.

To compare the two, I would like to reference a talk given by former president of Brigham Young University, Cecil O. Samuelson, titled, "What Does It Mean to Be Perfect?"

> Perfectionism is a medical condition characterized by severe self-criticism and self-doubt, often accompanied by anxiety, depression, or obsessive-compulsive behavior. It can lead to appetite and sleep disturbances, confusion, problems in relationships, inability to concentrate, procrastination of important tasks, and, if left untreated, major depression, anxiety disorders, and suicide.[1]

WHAT'S THE DIFFERENCE?

Doing Your Best	Perfectionism
You desire to give things your best efforts and are satisfied when you do.	You have a list of "shoulds" and "have to's" and are dissatisfied even if you complete them.
You know it's okay if you make a mistake. You move on and see your mistake as an opportunity for growth or learning.	Mistakes bring feelings of self-hatred. You don't want to do anything because you are afraid of failure.
You want to do your personal best, and you try not to compare your achievements to those of others. You don't need to be the best at all things.	You feel tremendous pressure to earn others' approval. You must be the best or "perfect" in your tasks.
You can find joy in doing the things you love, and you can get things accomplished.	Your need to do things perfectly leads to procrastination until you have time to do it "perfectly," and you feel driven by fear or duty instead of love.
Trying to do your best and perfecting yourself "line upon line" with the Savior's help is Christ-centered because you need the Atonement.	Perfectionism is self-centered. You measure yourself against your own standards and against others' standards, not God's.

So, how did this cultural myth of perfectionism get started?

I once attended a lecture series on grace at Brigham Young University and had the opportunity to hear from many scriptural experts, including Sheri Dew, Robert Millet, and Stephen Robinson.

For those unfamiliar with Stephen Robinson's work, he wrote the seminal book *Believing Christ*[2] and therein explained how a lot of us grow up believing *in* Christ, but not *believing* Christ. We believe that He performed His Atonement and that He can heal those who come to him, but it's different when it applies to our own circumstances. Simply put, He can forgive my friend, but He can't forgive me. When we not only believe *in* Christ but also *believe* Christ, we put our trust in Him when he tells us that, "I can get you where you need to be. Put your hand in mine and trust me."

I was in the audience as Brother Robinson gave his lecture on what grace is. He started by describing how many people in the Church culture have a hard time understanding grace because they think they need to be perfect in order to receive it, which is false. He used the pioneers as a possible breeding ground for this misunderstanding.

When the pioneers left Nauvoo, Winter Quarters, or wherever they were at the time, their instructions were very clear: complete the journey no matter what. Brigham Young couldn't say, "Now just go do your best, and if you die, the Lord will accept your efforts." They all would've died. He had to say, "You gotta get it done. You gotta make it. You gotta push through until you can't go any further." All works. No grace. And possibly, the pioneers took this philosophy and taught it to their children, who taught it to their children, and now it is the twenty-first century and we have this false notion within the Church that we receive absolutely no help until we have expended every last piece of energy and are depressed and miserable from pushing ourselves so hard.

Yes, the pioneers had to keep going or they would die. (Thank heavens for them all.) But we are different. We are not pioneers. We don't have to traverse prairies, fight cougars, or wade through snow that is up to our knees.

If the pioneers' challenges were mostly physical and spiritual, our challenges today are mostly emotional and spiritual. Neither challenge is greater than the other, yet they require different tools to get through.

You can't take someone with an emotional, social, or mental problem and throw a physical solution at them, such as repeatedly saying, "You gotta push through. You gotta endure. You gotta make it." It won't work.

We need to learn what types of problems we are suffering with and fit our solutions to those problems.

As President Gordon B. Hinckley so eloquently put it, "In all of living, have much fun and laughter. Life is to be enjoyed, not just endured."[3]

Now, you may think that those last paragraphs make sense, but your mind might immediately go to the scripture in 2 Nephi that says, "For we know that it is by grace that we are saved, after all we can do."

I think this scripture has caused more emotional breakdowns than any other. For me, it was very hard to understand. To be honest, it left me discouraged after reading it. I don't know about you, but when I think of "after all we can do," my mind goes to, "Okay, so I literally will not receive grace until I collapse from exhaustion, because that is what would happen if I did all I could do."

Anyone felt the same?

General conference was a week after I got home from the MTC, and, as I've mentioned numerous times throughout this book, I was having a difficult time coming to grips with the fact that I had done all I could do but was left with a feeling that my efforts were not good enough.

Then, Elder Dieter F. Uchtdorf gave a talk that changed my life. In his talk *The Gift of Grace*, he said,

> I wonder if sometimes we misinterpret the phrase "after all we can do." We must understand that "after" does not equal "because."
>
> We are not saved "because" of all we can do. Have any of us done *all* we can do? Does God wait until we've expended every effort before He will intervene in our lives with His saving grace?
>
> Many people feel discouraged because they constantly fall short. They know firsthand that "the spirit indeed is willing, but the flesh is weak." They raise their voices with Nephi in proclaiming, "My soul grieveth because of mine iniquities."
>
> I am certain Nephi knew that the Savior's grace *allows* and *enables* us to overcome sin. This is why Nephi labored so diligently to persuade his children and brethren "to believe in Christ, and to be reconciled to God."
>
> After all, *that is* what we can do! And *that is* our task in mortality.[4]

What is "all we can do"?
The answer is found in Alma 24:11–12.

> And now behold, my brethren, since it has been *all that we could do* (as we were the most lost of all mankind) to repent of all our sins and the many

murders which we have committed, and to get God to take them away from our hearts, for *it was all we could do to repent sufficiently* before God that he would take away our stain—

Now, my best beloved brethren, since God hath taken away our stains, and our swords have become bright, then let us stain our swords no more with the blood of our brethren (emphasis added).

We are to sufficiently repent before God of all our stains. That is all we can do.

One final note concerning grace: it may be better understood using an example that we are all familiar with, such as a mother and a newborn child. An overwhelming feeling of love is involved when a mother holds her new baby. The baby didn't do anything to earn that love, but the love is present. That's grace.

We may feel as though we won't receive grace until we *earn* it or *deserve* it; however, there is no mention of the words "earn" or "deserve" in the index or topical guide of the scriptures. We don't earn anything. We are forever indebted to Christ for what He did for us. We don't deserve Christ's love, but He gives it to us fully, completely, and perfectly. All we are asked is to do is repent sufficiently and rely on the Good Shepherd to guide us home again.

That is how we let go of the perfectionism within us. We realize that we are flawed beings. We accept it, receive the necessary help, and repent sufficiently of our sins. Then day by day, week by week, and month by month, we become better and better. And that is enough.

NOTES

1. Cecil O. Samuelson, "What Does It Mean to Be Perfect?," devotional, Mar. 19, 2002, Provo Missionary Training Center.
2. Stephen Robinson, *Believing Christ* (Salt Lake City: Bookcraft, 2010).
3. Gordon B. Hinckley, "Stand True and Faithful," *Ensign*, May 1996.
4. Dieter F. Uchtdorf, "The Gift of Grace," *Ensign*, May 2015.

CHAPTER 11

A SISTER'S PERSPECTIVE

A mission is a very personal experience. It is an experience shared between you and the Lord. This chapter is devoted strictly to a sister's perspective of missionary service and how God can guide women in their lives to make decisions that are right for them. It is for sisters who may feel pressure to serve missions but aren't quite sure if they want to, sisters who want to serve missions but don't know what to expect, and sisters who didn't serve missions and feel left out or "lesser" because of their decision.

My wife has kindly allowed me to share her story. She grew up in a family of ten children—five were adopted, and five were biological children of their parents. She was adopted from the country of Kazakhstan when she was three by two loving, respectable, and generous parents. Though she grew up as a member of The Church of Jesus Christ of Latter-day Saints, she never had the desire to serve a mission. She went throughout her junior high and high school years with one dream: to get married and become a mother. She knew her mission in life was to raise a family of her own and didn't think a full-time mission was necessary tutorage in preparing for this dream. In fact, when the missionary age was lowered for young women, she didn't feel the need to go at all.

Can anyone relate?

As she entered her senior year in high school, she was attending seminary one day when her teacher stood in front of the class and openly asked those who planned to serve a mission to raise their hands. All hands in the classroom went up—except for my wife's. Because this question is so personal, it should be asked with discretion, especially in a large audience where some may feel left out or ostracized because of their decision to be in the minority. Since my wife didn't raise her hand, the teacher proceeded to say these words in a persuasive way: "You know, ladies, serving a mission will make you a better wife and mother one day."

My wife was shocked. She raised her hand and blatantly told the teacher in front of the entire class that he shouldn't say things like that, first, because that statement is untrue, and second, because there are many wonderful women who don't serve missions who turn out to be great wives and mothers.

Success as a wife and mother isn't conditional upon a young lady serving a mission for The Church of Jesus Christ of Latter-day Saints.

When members of the Church make statements such as my wife's seminary teacher made, regardless of how well intended they are, they are spreading false cultural stigmas that others might accept as doctrine. It's not doctrine; it's cultural. Of course women can learn amazing things on a mission that might help them in becoming a better wife and mother. However, just as there is more than one way for a woman to find a job and earn a living, there is more than one way for a woman to learn key attributes that will serve her in preparing for her role as a wife and mother.

What's the difference between cultural pressure and noncultural pressure?

Cultural Pressure Examples

1. You know, you'd be a better wife and mother if you served a mission.
2. I know many guys who will want to date you because you served a mission.
3. If you don't serve a mission, you won't be as prepared for life's trials.

Noncultural Pressure examples

1. Regardless of what you decide to do, I am 100 percent supportive of you.
2. I can't tell you what you should or shouldn't do, but I know the Lord has a plan for you, and if you pray and listen to Him, you'll make the right decision.
3. With the Lord's help, decide which it will be: school and work or start your mission papers. You'll know which is right for you by how you feel when you are pursuing it.

Though these cultural and non-cultural examples vary, I hope you can see the overall differences. No one likes being pressured to do something, regardless of where they come from or what gender they are. It's not our place to make decisions for people or to coerce them into a decision for our personal benefit. That isn't the plan of happiness, and it doesn't lead to growth. When it comes to decisions of possible eternal significance, we encourage people to speak with the Lord about it. He is the only one with the key to every heart. Then they must decide for themselves.

My mother didn't serve a mission, yet she is the most Christlike woman I've ever known. My sisters didn't serve missions, yet they possess traits I would associate with divinity. Most of my sisters-in-law didn't serve missions, yet what they have accomplished in their lives is astronomical. They each have a work ethic and determination to succeed unlike anything I've ever seen.

We need to stop applying cultural pressure to young women to serve missions, whether we are dating them, are family to them, or are their friends.

In the prophetic words of Jeffrey R. Holland,

> [We] never intended for all of the young women in the Church to go on missions by dropping [the] age [to 19]. We're very grateful for those who go. It's changed the face of the Church. . . . But we do not want anyone feeling inadequate or left out or undignified or tarnished because she did not choose to serve a mission. And we're a little irritated with young men who say, "Well, I'm not going to date you because you didn't serve a mission." . . . We do not want that kind of climate over dating or marriages. . . . It isn't our place to pass a judgment.[1]

It isn't our place to pass a judgment.

Getting back to my wife's story, as one could probably guess, this experience in seminary only strengthened her desire to *not* serve a mission.

A few months went by, and every now and again, the question would come up: "Sabrina, are you going to serve a mission when you turn nineteen?"

Each time the question came up, my wife would respectfully say, "I've been thinking about it, but I'm not sure yet," while in her mind she was thinking, *Stop asking me if I'm going to serve a mission. It's none of your business, and the more you keep asking me, the more I don't want to.*

In fact, there was one person in her life that was applying so much pressure on her to serve a mission that one day Sabrina told him, "If you keep pressuring me to serve a mission, I'll never go. So, stop pressuring me."

This stopped the pressure, but this person still wanted Sabrina to talk to her bishop about it and get some advice.

So, as the end of her senior year approached, Sabrina decided to talk to her bishop so that *he* would tell her she didn't have to serve a mission. At least this would provide for her a legit excuse when she told people why she wasn't going on a mission . . . but when she met with him, she got a different answer.

She sat down with him, and they had a short conversation about serving a mission. The bishop, to his eternal credit, said something along the lines of, "You know, Sabrina, if you don't want to go on a mission, that's just fine; but I do want you to pray about it and see what the Spirit guides you to do."

Sabrina, though she was bummed out that the bishop didn't tell her directly she didn't have to serve a mission, took his advice.

For the first couple of months, her prayers were insincere and thus inconsequential. She didn't want to serve a mission, so why would she pray faithfully about it?

Her life went on, but as we've seen throughout the experiences shared in this book, the Lord is in the details. Piece by piece, and little by little, she started including more spiritual teachings in her life. She finished the Book of Mormon. She started praying with more sincerity, and she focused on listening to the Spirit's direction. She started praying sincerely about whether serving a mission for The Church of Jesus Christ of Latter-day Saints was right for her personal circumstance. She got an answer.

She went back to the bishop later that year and told him she wanted to serve a mission. . . .

Yes, you read that right. The girl who didn't raise her hand in seminary, who would cringe when people asked her if she was serving a mission, and who never *desired* to serve a full-time mission, had developed the desire to serve a mission.)

The bishop looked at her with a calm smile and said, "I always knew you would decide to serve a mission. I just knew the decision had to be between you and the Lord. A decision as personal as this can't be made correctly when a lot of pressure is applied."

A lot of cultural pressure is applied to the women in the Church to do many things, such as serve a mission, work or don't work, get married at a specific time, have children at a specific time, and so on. Sabrina wanted every sister reading this to know, without a doubt, what really matters is that you ask the Lord to help you make the right decision for *you* and *your* circumstances. His voice will never lead you astray.

My wife was called to serve the Lord and was assigned to labor in the Florida Tallahassee Mission. She loved her full-time mission. It was perfect for *her*. She learned how to love people that she never thought she could love. She learned to rely on the Lord for strength and answers to prayers. She learned that regardless of the storms that were swirling around her, she could feel peace and love, because she is a daughter of loving Heavenly Parents.

Her mission experience was personal to her. It may be similar to your circumstance, but it may be the exact opposite, and both are perfectly fine. She went from having zero desire to serve a mission, to talking about it almost every day because of the positive impact it had on her. What made the difference?

She stopped focusing on all the well-intentioned (but loud) voices outside of her and listened to the still, small voice inside of her.

Whether it be to serve a mission for The Church of Jesus Christ of Latter-day Saints, to take a service trip with your local community, to accept a certain job you've been considering, when you should get married, if it's right to have one more child, what to study in college, if you should go back to college, and so on—make your decision with the Lord's help. Listen to your parents, listen to your leaders, listen to your friends, but ultimately, listen to the Lord and follow Him. Your *mission* may be to serve a full-time mission. It may be to get married. It may be to go to school and study. It may be to live at home and work to save money. It could be anything, and that's the point of this book, to help you discover the meaning of *your* mission.

Regardless of what your mission is, the Lord loves you and He knows your heart. He knows what is right for you. Try not to compare yourself to those around you. They have their own missions to fulfill.

You are special. You are beyond beautiful, and your life will be what you make of it. You are enough.

NOTES

1. Jeffrey R. Holland, Face to Face broadcast, Mar. 8, 2016. See facetoface.lds.org. Accessed June 17, 2020.

CHAPTER 12

YOUR MISSION AWAITS YOU

It is my prayer that throughout this book you've been able to see how the Lord works in mysterious ways to bring to pass his eternal purposes. As one could probably guess, I never did return to the mission field as a full-time missionary. The Lord reassigned me, and just like each person on this earth, my mission was unique to me.

After I had been home about eighteen months, I received word from my sister-in-law that BYU had just announced that for the first time, students could go to the Baltic States to participate in an internship of their choice. Simply put, whoever wanted to pay the tuition, applied, and was accepted into this program had the opportunity to go to Estonia, Latvia, or Lithuania and participate in a summer internship. I couldn't believe what I was hearing, so I quickly picked up the phone and dialed the number for the college dean. Miraculously, he answered. (I say miraculously, because each time I called him back after that first phone call, he wasn't in his office.)

We had a brief talk and hung up on the same page: I was to send him my resume and where I wanted to intern in Estonia, and he would accept me into the program. Then we would go from there.

At the time, I was studying neuroscience, with the hopes of being a psychiatrist and aiding missionaries who had come home early, so naturally, I decided to intern in the Estonian hospitals.

Little did I know that I would be the first American intern (since the country gained its independence) to serve with the doctors in the hospitals there.

Yes, the Lord had a plan for me, and yes, He has a plan for each of us.

Long story short, BYU set up the entire internship: when I would arrive, where I would live, what days and times I would be in various medical departments, and when I would come home.

The remainder of my time was up to me.

It ended up being the greatest gift God could ever give me in terms of serving a *mission*. I got to learn the language, speak the language, serve the people, go to Church, help the missionaries, participate in autopsies (yes, you read that right), embryology, cataract surgeries (just watching), and was blessed with the opportunity to share the gospel with a doctor who became a dear friend. (By the way, that friend never came to Church or was baptized, but that doesn't matter. What does matter is the friendship we cultivated and the opportunity we had to share what was in our hearts.)

Yes, the Lord had a plan for me. No, it wasn't my *original* plan, or even my *back-up* plan, but it was the *right* plan.

The Lord knew that if I had been in Estonia with a black name tag on and wearing a suit, I wouldn't have had the experiences I personally needed to serve and learn from Him. That doesn't mean that all the other missionaries there weren't in the *right* place. Absolutely they were. They were called to serve their own individual missions, and I am positive they had the exact experiences the Lord intended for them to have.

The Lord knows you. He knows your needs. He knows what your *mission* is supposed to be. He knows where you need to be and when you need to be there. We need to listen, take one step at a time, and trust Him.

It may take years for us to connect the dots and see God's hand, but it will stand as a witness to His love, matchless power, and perfect timing.

I didn't write this book for formal missionaries who came home early for one reason or another, though I understand their pain. I didn't even write this book for full-time missionaries in general. I wrote it for anyone who might be struggling with his or her self-worth or identity. I wrote it for anyone who might be struggling with cultural stigmas or nondoctrinal challenges. I wrote it for those who want to serve God and are doing the best they can, but for one reason or another, they just don't feel like they or their service matters. I wrote it for anyone who may be wondering, "What is my mission in life?" My experience as a missionary for The Church of Jesus Christ of Latter-day Saints opened my eyes to the problems this culture struggles with and how we need to help those who don't feel wanted or welcomed, regardless of their circumstances or where they are with their testimonies. I hope my story has inspired you to be a little kinder, empathize a little more, and live the gospel a little better, knowing that you can learn and accomplish your mission in life. If people around you are judgmental of your decision to discover and live out your own mission, smile at them and say, "Thank you for your concern, but I'm not doing it for you."

No matter your circumstances in life, trust in the Lord. Fear not. Pour out your heart to Him, and then listen for what He asks you to do next . . . then do it. Miracles will follow.

I am living proof that the Lord answers prayers and guides our steps, perhaps not in the way we would like, but in the way that is best for us. *Grow* through the persecution, *grow* through the judgments, *grow* through the trials, and know that the Lord is with you, for the only opinion that truly matters is His.

In case you're wondering, I'm not a doctor, though I thought I would be after my internship. The Lord knew my heart and my future and has helped me find something even better for my personal circumstances. I work as a publicity manager for a leadership development firm and love what I do.

Remember: You didn't come this far to only come this far. Keep going, do your best, and the Lord will accept and bless your effort. Your mission awaits you!

AUTHOR'S NOTE

Many sources are available if you need help: your family, your bishop, or a gospel-oriented professional counselor. If professional assistance is needed or you want to find out more about perfectionism, go to ldsfamilyservices .org. To learn more about how to become perfect without being a perfectionist, read "Perfection Pending," President Russell M. Nelson, *Ensign,* Nov. 1995, 86.

ABOUT THE AUTHOR

Drew Young is a native of the east coast, growing up in Connecticut. He now resides in Utah with his wife and daughter.

Drew studied at Brigham Young University where he was actively involved in teaching and developing curriculum for various student development courses. He's been sharing his story with numerous audiences around Salt Lake County for the past five years and has been featured in LDS Living's YouTube series and magazine.

He serves as the publicity manager at FranklinCovey, where he assists in managing best-selling book launches and social media

campaigns, as well as booking high-profile thought leaders, storytellers, and celebrities for *On Leadership*, the fastest growing and largest leadership development online newsletter in the world.

To contact Drew to speak at an event (or to just say "hello"), please visit his website at drewbyoung.com. He can also be reached at mrdrewbyoung (Instagram) and mrdrewbyoung1 (Facebook).

Scan to visit

drewbyoung.com